THE COMPLETE MANAGER'S GUIDE TO INTERVIEWING: HOW TO HIRE THE BEST

THE COMPLETE MANAGER'S GUIDE TO INTERVIEWING: HOW TO HIRE THE BEST

ARTHUR H. BELL, Ph.D.
Georgetown University

Dow Jones-Irwin
Homewood, Illinois 60430

Dow Jones-Irwin is a trademark of Dow Jones & Company, Inc.

This publication is designed to provide accurate and authoritative
information in regard to the subject matter covered. It is sold
with the understanding that the publisher is not engaged in
rendering legal, accounting, or other professional service. If
legal advice or other expert assistance is required, the services
of a competent professional person should be sought.

*From a Declaration of Principles jointly adopted by a Committee
of the American Bar Association and a Committee of Publishers.*

Sponsoring editor: Jim Childs
Project editor: Jane Lightell
Production manager: Stephen K. Emry
Designer: Reneé Klyczek
Compositor: Publication Services, Inc.
Typeface: 11/13 Times Roman
Printer: The Book Press

Library of Congress Cataloging-in-Publication Data

Bell, Arthur H. (Arthur Henry), 1946–
    The complete manager's guide to interviewing.
    Includes index.
    1. Employment interviewing.   I. Title.
HF5549.5.I6B397   1989   658.3'1124   88–29963
JSBN 1-55623-109-1

Printed in the United States of America

2 3 4 5 6 7 8 9 0   BP   5 4 3 2 1 0

Dedicated with affection to
Robert, Charles, and Julie Bell

INTRODUCTION

Is this book for you? Answer that questions by taking a 10-question quiz. Do you know. . .

What kinds of questions to ask in an interview?

The latest legal restrictions and guidelines on interview questions?

How to record interview results for effective decision-making?

How to use scorable tests in interviews?

If and how to use drug testing and questions related to drug use?

Verbal and nonverbal techniques for getting the most out of your interviewee?

How to choose the best location for the interview?

How how to probe for facts and feelings?

How to recognize and control interviewer bias?

How to practice active listening?

The Complete Manager's Guide to Interviewing answers these questions in practical ways for both beginning and experienced interviewers at all levels within the company.

TABLE OF CONTENTS

Key Words.   Beginnings of New Topics.   Summaries.
Conclusions.   PAUSES.   ARTICULATION.   PITCH.
PUTTING IMPROVEMENTS INTO PRACTICE.

CHAPTER 5   NONVERBAL TECHNIQUES FOR INTERVIEWING   54

THE HEART OF THE MATTER: CAN NONVERBAL
BEHAVIOR BE CONTROLLED?   EYE CONTACT.
ACHIEVING GOOD EYE CONTACT.   AN EYE
CONTACT EXPERIMENT.   Other Uses of Eye
Contact.   POSTURE AND BODY MOVEMENT.
FACIAL EXPRESSIONS.   DRESS.   Thou Shalt
Not Embarrass the Company.   Thou Shalt Not
Peacock Thyself.   Thou Shalt Not Wilt.   Thou
Shalt Not Judge Interviewees Only by Their Threads.
Thou Shalt Plan Clothes in Advance.   A PLEA ON
BEHALF OF NATURALNESS.

CHAPTER 6   ACTIVE LISTENING FOR INTERVIEWING   68

TYPES OF LISTENING.   Free-for-all Listening.
Listening for Facts.   Objective Listening for
Attitudes and Feelings.   Empathetic Listening
for Attitudes and Feelings.   BARRIERS TO
EFFECTIVE LISTENING.   Poor Listening Due to Prior
Assumptions.   Poor Listening Due to Emotional
Interference.   Poor Listening Due to Competition.
TECHNIQUES FOR ACTIVE LISTENING.   Nip Your
Daydreams.   Make Connections.   Mentally Talk
Back to the Candidate.   Pick Out Key Words.
Check Your Comprehension by Feedback.   Be
Comfortable with Silence.   THREE LISTENING
EXERCISES.   Nightly News.   Your Significant
Other.   What They Do Well.   Insert: A
Potpourri of Poor Listeners

Questions from a Resume or Application Form.
STAGE FOUR. DEVELOP A WAY TO RECORD
IMPORTANT ASPECTS OF APPLICANTS'
RESPONSES. The Weighted Evaluation Form.
The Importance of Record Keeping. STAGE
FIVE. ARRANGE QUESTIONS IN A BALANCED
SEQUENCE. Structured Interviews. Nondirective
Interviews. A Typical Sequence of Interview
Activities. STAGE SIX. TEST THE INTERVIEW
PLAN. STAGE SEVEN. TRAIN INTERVIEWERS
TO USE THE INTERVIEW PLAN. STAGE EIGHT.
TRY THE INTERVIEW PLAN ON REAL
APPLICANTS. SPECIAL CONSIDERATIONS IN
QUESTIONS INVOLVING DRUGS.
Insert: The Corporate Selection Cycle

THE INTENT OF THE NEW LAWS. Race or Color.
Citizenship. Family and Marital Status. Sex and
Sexual Preference. Handicaps and Health-related
Issues. Age. Religion. Application Forms
Employment Testing. The Construction of a Valid
Test. State Laws. How a Disgruntled Applicant
Proves Discrimination. SUMMING UP.

The Challenge Probe. The Amplification/
Clarification Probe. The Conclusionary Probe.
The Investigative Probe. CONTROLLING
TOPICS AND MAKING TRANSITIONS.
Maintaining Control. Controlling the
Sequence of Topics. Controlling Length
of Responses. Dealing with Resistance.
Dealing with Hostility. CONCLUDING THE
INTERVIEW AND FOLLOWING UP. Conclusionary

Signals.   What Is Included in a Conclusion?
What to Do Once the Interview Is Over.

CHAPTER 1

INTERVIEWING IS
YOUR BUSINESS

Hour for hour, nothing an employee does is more valuable or more expensive for the company than interviewing. Selection interviews, for example, are the sensitive growth tip of the company—the place where, as the aerospace company, TRW, proclaims, "the future is taking place today." Through the lifeline of interviews and hiring, a company perpetuates, repairs, rejuvenates, and sometimes revolutionizes itself.

Other types of interviews form the spreading roots of the company—the system of "connections" without which business itself would wither. In interviews for negotiation, counseling, information exchange, problem solving, and other purposes, coworkers reenact the original meaning of *interview*— shared seeing, mutual insight.

Expensive? You bet. In managerial time alone, American business spent approximately $26 billion in 1987 preparing for, conducting, and evaluating interviews. Add to that the interview-related expense of personnel staff, secretaries, employment ads, recordkeeping, and "hospitality." According to the American Management Association, it can cost $50,000 to find and relocate a manager for an $80,000 job. In a 1980 survey, 25 percent of companies spent at least $1,000 to hire a new man or woman for sales, with 50 percent spending between $1,000 and $5,000.

Companies pay in other ways for the interview process. While key managers conduct interviews, important projects sit on hold. The information flow and the decision-making process in the company cramp up. Why? "Ms. Evans is tied up in interviews today, and has asked not to be disturbed."

Unfortunately, companies also pay the price of inefficient, ineffective interviewing. The cost of a bad hire, comments Fred Smith, sales manager for Quad Systems, "is not found on an income statement, nor was it budgeted, at least not entirely. Turnover costs include the cost of lost production, . . . employment advertising, recruiting fees, training, and possibly severance, outplacement and unemployment insurance. Then there are the hidden costs of time — time to discipline, document performance, terminate, write and place ads, recruit, screen applicants, interview and train."[1]

As recently reported in *Fortune*, "an employee who flops and leaves after a few months can cost a company anywhere from $5,000 for an hourly worker to $75,000 for a manager in lost productivity and money spent on training. The cost may be even greater if you hire the wrong person and he or she stays on, making mistakes and sabotaging morale." The general rule of thumb, states human resources expert Dr. Kurt Einstein, is "that an average selection error costs your organization a minimum of two times that individual's annual salary."

To make matters worse, business captains have not-so-steady hands on the tillers of ships heading into uncharted waters. In the last decade of the twentieth century, interviewing for American companies will face five critical realities.

1. More Interviews Than Ever Before

Owing in part to Equal Employment Opportunity (EEO) requirements as well as a more participatory style of management, companies will see more job candidates more often. Well over half of American managers, according to recent surveys, personally interview potential new hires. Many companies have a multitiered interview process. At Minnesota Mutual successful candidates go through no less than five interviews in addition to psychological evaluation. At American Tool & Die four interviews are routinely conducted, with more for management positions. At Trammel Crow Co., the country's largest real estate developer, candidates for management positions go through not only interviews with two or three top partners but also with

---

[1]Individuals quoted in this book are listed in alphabetical order at the end of the book.

secretaries or field agents. According to McDonald Williams, managing partner at Trammel Crow, if the candidate "is incongruent, we know we'll have problems later on."

Other forms of interviews, particularly the exit interview, will increase almost exponentially in number as companies recognize their value and as employees change jobs more often. By U.S. Department of Labor estimates, one-half of all newly hired people will not last more than six months in the positions for which they were hired. And those who remain are changing jobs more often. In 1963 the typical worker kept his or her job for an average of 4.6 years. By 1987 that figure across industries had dropped to less than 3 years.

At the same time, more jobs are available than ever before. Bureau of Labor Statistics economist Jon Sargent projects that in the period from 1988 to 1995 the number of jobs requiring a college degree will increase 45 percent—three times the growth rate projected for all jobs in the U.S. economy. These are precisely the positions that require the most time, expense, and company effort in the interviewing process.

2. Job Descriptions Are Changing

In the last decade of the twentieth century, companies will increasingly find themselves trying to hit a moving target with regard to hiring. Under the stress of mergers, acquisitions, reorganization, technological change, market expansion or redefinition, companies know less and less exactly what they want in an employee. They will be hiring more for breadth of experience and insight rather than specific skills. It goes without saying that the interview techniques necessary to locate such individuals will differ drastically from the cookie-cutter interviews of the past.

Big retail chains have been especially aggressive in beating the bushes for good hires. As reported in *Forbes*, Jordan Marsh planned to interview 1,400 students in 1986 to fill 200 jobs. Macy's interviewed 7,000 applicants for 600 positions. The May Company planned to visit 75 colleges and interview 3,700 students before hiring 350 trainees. The recruiting effort can be deft. "They send recent alumni back to a school to act as talent scouts. They make it a point to talk to key faculty members and administrators to find out who the top students are," says University of Virginia's career planning director Larry Simpson, who regularly provides retailers with mailing lists of "1800 or 2000 people they might send invitations to."

3. Employees Are Changing

Where do you find good candidates for company training as computer programmers?   Among English majors, say executives at Control Data, Computer Automation, and elsewhere. What one course is a necessity for premed students, according to the Medical School at the University of California, San Diego? Shakespeare. The "get'em from trade tech" approach to recruiting has passed. Companies have learned to value a candidate's wide range of experience and interest. As a straw in the wind, notice how few "must haves" are now listed in classified job ads for white collar positions. Laurie Winthrop, vice president and regional product personnel manager for 12 Macy's stores, interviews 200 or so applicants a year. She breaks her list of desired qualifications "into two columns: 'criticals' and 'nice-to-haves'. Decide what is essential and what you can live without."

Probably the biggest single change in employee attitudes is a new entrepreneurial spirit toward managing one's own career growth. According to National Personnel Associates, the recruiting network, an estimated 29 percent of employed managers and 34 percent of employed technicians have resumes circulating. Comments industrial psychologist Arthur A. Witkin, "employers who fail to recognize that five jobs in seven years is not necessarily a sign of instability may be disqualifying today's best applicants."

4. Reward Systems Are Changing

Potential employees come to the modern interview as much to get as to give. They want to find out what the company "feels" like from the inside, what its people say about it, and what they can expect besides money. When Amy DiGeso was lured away from Estée Lauder, Inc., to become vice president of human resources at Banker's Trust Company, she credited "the little things that make a difference, that influence the way a person feels about a company." For her, the pro-employee attitude at Banker's Trust shone in her interviews. "Even in this resource-short, competitive market," she says, "some companies act as if they're the only ones making the decision. It's a mutual decision."

As statistical summaries of exit surveys clearly demonstrate, employees care about human factors as much as financial factors in assessing their employment. A survey reported in *Personnel*, May 1985, shows that, at the time they left, 38 percent of employees pointed to salary and benefits as the primary reasons for departure. When interviewed 18 months later, that number had dropped to 12 percent. The 4 percent of employees who previously said they left "for supervision reasons" leaped to 24 percent in the later interview.

If money alone can't attract and hold good employees, companies must look to a more basic resource—their people. When Sandra Meyer left her position as marketing manager for General Foods' coffee division to become president of the communications division of American Express, the people she met in the interview process made the difference. "I was excited intellectually by the man who wanted to hire me. He presented the business in a very exciting way and talked about product-line issues. It was a very smart way to appeal to me. Fascinating man, complex business."

Writing in the *Personnel Journal*, Arthur Witkin sums up the matter: "Salary and security were the paramount requirements until a few years ago. They have been replaced by job satisfaction, responsibility, recognition, sensitive supervision, and related wants. This is particularly true for the better educated and more highly motivated employees. Managers who expect obeisance during interviews are unrealistic."

5. Social Needs and Values Are Changing

The John Wayne approach to interviewing—to hell with the rules, pilgrim—no longer rides tall in the saddle. Companies are constrained by law and often motivated by social conscience to interview with an eye toward racial and sexual balance. Interviewers are warned to beware of taboo topics—religion, plans for children, and so forth. Elaborate records are maintained not only to substantiate why a candidate was hired but also to show why other candidates were turned down. "Sunshine" legislation has made even the writing of a letter of recommendation legally hazardous.

THE BOTTOM LINE

It's little wonder, then, that the interview hasn't been a star performer in finding Mr. or Ms. Right. As summarized by Wayne F. Cascio in *Applied Psychology in Personnel Management* (Reston, 1982), 30 years of research indicate that the interview as conducted in American business, when compared to other selection procedures, has little or no value in predicting employee success. The main reasons are well summed up by Robert Zawacki in *Datamation*, September 1985.

- Interviewers tend to develop a stereotype of a good candidate and then seem to match applicants with stereotypes.
- Biases are established early in the interview.
- During an interview in which the applicant is accepted, the interviewer talks more and in a more favorable tone than in an interview in which the applicant is rejected.
- Interviewers are influenced more by unfavorable than by favorable information.
- Seeing negative candidates before positive candidates will result in a greater number of favorable acceptances than the other way around.
- There are reliable and consistent individual differences among interviewers in determining judgments; this increases, not decreases, with interviewing experience.
- Early impressions are crystallized after a mean interview time of only four minutes.
- The ability of a candidate to respond concisely, to answer questions fully, to state personal opinions when relevant, and to keep to the subject at hand appears to be crucial to obtaining a favorable employment decision.
- Interviewers benefit very little from day-to-day interviewing experience.
- An interviewer who begins an interview with an unfavorable expectancy may tend to give an applicant less credit for past accomplishments and ultimately may be more likely to decide that the applicant is unacceptable.

The challenge is obvious: American business has in place, up and running, an incredibly expensive interviewing system that just isn't working. Against the foreboding backdrop of new legal stakes, changing social priorities, new technologies, and organizational structures, this book offers a guide for the players. It discusses all major aspects of interviewing, with specific treatment of the 20 most common types of interviews.

Its goal: to help you use interviewing as a cost-efficient, reliable tool for decision making and communication.

CHAPTER 2

INTERVIEWERS AND
THEIR MANY HATS

Few of us take along enough hats for the changing climate of the modern interview. Reflect for a moment on the complex, shifting current of activities taking place there.

• **Establishing a Relationship.** Often in half an hour or less you're expected to get a relationship off on the right foot—and not only a personal relationship ("Hi, George, I'm Alice Parker") but also a budding relationship between the candidate and the company. That's a tall order for such a limited time span, especially when dealing with a nervous candidate and somewhat stressful questions.

Keeping good employees begins with the interview relationship, points out Vincent F. Brennan, vice president at Korn/Ferry International. "People don't just work for money. They need that warm and fuzzy feeling that they're cared about."

• **Collecting Information.** The candidate comes prepared to "dump" dozens of items of information on you—past jobs, past experiences, present abilities, future aspirations. Often these come rapid fire, in no particular order. You, as interviewer, are expected to catch whatever the cadidate pitches—all the while maintaining rapport, asking questions, showing interest, and so forth. A court reporter would be challenged to collect the information you're expected to record. To add insult to injury, virtually all interviewing guides warn against "obtrusive" notetaking.

• **Guiding Conversation.** You have areas you want to cover. (You've probably given the candidate an overview of those areas from the beginning.) One of your most difficult tasks, then, is keeping the interview on course and on schedule, with various portions given appropriate amounts of time. You're participating in conversation with that same rapt attention a psychiatrist uses toward the end of

the 50-minute hour—one ear for the candidate and one for the inner alarm clock: "That's extremely interesting, but we should move on."
• **Probing.** You want the interview to give you more than a resume or tape recording could. Therefore, you "dig" a bit here and there to clarify facts, uncover additional information, and invite disclosure on the part of the candidate. You're spending energy not only thinking of appropriate ways to phrase your probing questions but also evaluating your emotional tone: Will the question sound hostile, suspicious, or picky? Worse, will your probe reveal that you haven't heard what a candidate has already told you?

The key, says human resources expert Dr. Kurt Einstein, is to "listen to and interpret what a candidate would rather not tell you, which is the most important information you need to make an objective decision."
• **Interpreting Facts, Representations, and Feelings.** In your microseconds of "free time," you're supposed to be assembling an accurate mirror of the candidate from the flying shards of conversation. He worked with mainframe computers, but not micros. So what? She supervised four people, all of them older women. What does this tell you? He's held four jobs in five years. A positive? A negative? What goes on inside the interviewer's head can come to sound like a ping-pong game, with the candidate continually throwing more and more balls onto the table. The difficulty, of course, is the "English" on the balls—the unexpected quirks, spins, and curves as you distinguish fact from representation. All the while, feelings— yours and the candidate's—are influencing how you evaluate what's being said.
• **Recording Information and Judgments.** Your company knows your hands have not been busy during the interview and, there- fore, provides an interview scoresheet you're expected to fill out in the heat of the chase. These sheets can be complex, asking you to record everything from the candidate's demeanor ("Confident?" "Friendly?") to graduation and employment dates. The stakes for thoroughness and accuracy are high: federal and state laws require "observable" and "preservable" data supporting your person- nel decisions, particularly when Affirmative Action guidelines are concerned.
• **Giving Information.** The interview is a two-way street. You and your company are being appraised at the same time you are evaluating the candidate. During the interview, therefore, you must

give out information about the company. Much of this information is predictable: benefit plans, current projects, future prospects. But you must also be prepared to deal with unexpected questions—those from 'left field' that can make or break a candidate's view of the company. "On average, how many promotions are made from my job level to the next level each year?" An equivocating "I'm not sure, but quite a few" will seem evasive. Part of preparing to give information is to have information not only at the tip of your tongue, but also at the tip of your fingers in the form of manuals, information summaries, and employee handbooks. You may not want to take time during the interview to look up a fact or figure. But a reassuring pat on a fat book—"Let's check the exact figures when we're done"—can make your case without breaking your pace.

• **Creating Impressions**. Your face, your dress, your posture, your words, your silences—all these and more create impressions for the interviewee. In one of the classic "hard sells" of all time, Steve Jobs of Apple Computer persuaded David Scully, then president of Pepsico, to come aboard as chief executive officer. Scully recalls that it was Jobs himself—his enthusiasm, his sense of mission, his irreverence—that eventually persuaded the Pepsico chief to switch. Jobs took significant risks, by the way, in creating impressions for Scully. After being turned down for what Jobs feared was the the last time, he paused for a long moment, then said to Scully, "Do you really want to sell sugar water for the rest of your life?"

All these internal and external activities are going on at once in the skilled interviewer during a selection interview. "I've had many different job responsibilities during my career," says past Safeway CEO Dale Lynch, "and they all come back to me when I interview someone." Consider the career hats an interviewer carries into the interview situation.

THE DETECTIVE

In virtually all types of interviews you must be prepared to probe beneath surface appearances in search of the truth. Like a detective, you are constantly collecting and assembling clues—a reservation here, an exaggeration there, a hesitation or a show of temper. These are the materials by which you turn raw data into that far more valuable commodity, meaning.

The Detective at Work

> Q. You smiled when you mentioned your former boss. Anything there you want to share?
>
> A. (chuckles) He was a funny guy. He just couldn't stand competition, you know? Had to have everyone under his thumb.
>
> Q. You felt pushed around?
>
> A. Well, I didn't because I wouldn't let him. But everyone else did.
>
> Q. How did you react to his management style?
>
> A. I just went around him, if you know what I mean. There are a thousand ways you can let a boss know you're not going to take any crap.
>
> Q. Such as?
>
> A. (begins to clam up) Well, nothing special. Actually, we got along fairly well once I let him know my limits.

(Interviewer makes note to review candidate's relations with superiors.)

As Detective, the interviewer must keep up with both federal and state legislation guiding what can and can't be asked. In addition to knowing the law (an in-depth discussion can be found in Chapter 9), the interviewer must be able to apply the law to his or her own questions, comments, and procedures. In the landmark *Griggs vs. Duke Power* Supreme Court ruling, the justices ruled that a job candidate was unfairly discriminated against by having him take a pencil-and-paper test, when such writing skills would not be part of his work tasks. Other "hot spots" involve plans for children, religious or political associations, and some aspects of citizenship.

The most effective "detective" questions occur within a context of rapport rather than "cat and mouse." Interviewees who sense that the interviewer is attempting to trip them up will resort to game playing of their own: half-truths, overstatement, and defensive posturing.

THE MERCHANT

Especially in selection interviews, the company is sending the interviewer on an explicit buying trip. He or she is expected to examine the goods and bring home the bacon. (A manager's career, in fact, often rises or falls based on the soundness of hiring decisions.)

The psychology of buying occurs daily, usually in these stages.

First, we find the right source so as not to waste our time. Second, we decide whether chill or charm will prove most advantageous in our bargain making. If our aloofness will bring price concessions and a "let-me-do-more-for-you" attitude on the part of the buyer, we can show a frozen face and give out ice cube words with the best of them. If, on the other hand, we feel that charm will grease the wheels of business, we can pour warm fuzzies over the transaction from the beginning. Third, we firm up goods and terms. Precisely what we're getting—no b.s.—and what we're paying is agreed upon.

We consciously or unconsciously employ that essential merchant psychology in selection interviews. What adds zest to the process, of course, is that a double game is being played. From the interviewee's point of view, he or she is trying to buy a job by flashing a wad of education and experience. The "moves" in the double merchant game pass back and forth quickly. But the skilled interviewer never loses control as buyer. In other words, the interviewer takes a proactive, "we-want-the-best" attitude rather than a reactive, "we-have-something-to-offer" perspective. The Kingston Trio said it best: "I'd rather be a hammer than a nail."

The Merchant at Work

> Q. As we discussed on the phone, this company is looking for a rare person—someone with computer expertise and word skills. Tell me about the lab manual you wrote as a teaching assistant.
>
> A. Well, at State University our mainframe had quite a few quirks that weren't covered in standard programming textbooks. I organized all of these special cases into a manual which was published by the university. It's still being used, I think.
>
> Q. Do you like to do such technical writing?
>
> A. I love it, probably because it comes easy to me. Once you understand some new technology, it's satisfying to be able to explain it to others.
>
> Q. Have you had a chance to look at our user manuals?
>
> A. Yes. In general, I think that (the interviewee goes on to discuss the manuals).

Notice the "Merchant" pattern followed in this dialogue. The interviewer states what the company is looking for, then begins squeezing the tomatoes, so to speak, in search of Mr. or Ms. Right. How different and how less effective this interview would have been if the interviewer had taken of position of Producer rather Buyer: "What kind of job interests you?" The interviewee now takes on the Merchant role, setting forth the ground rules of the transaction.

THE JUDGE

In many interview situations, you sit as judge and jury over a candidate's professional future with the company. Rarely is there a route of appeal—your verdict ("He's too withdrawn") is final.

In such an absolute environment, you, no less than a court judge, must adhere to a firm sense of personal ethics and beware of personal bias. The obvious biases—race, religion, and so forth—we'll assume are under control. It's the subtle biases that too often let good employees slip through a company's fingers and into the courts. Here's a shopping list of such biases.

The Bothersome Habit
She smacks her lips before speaking. He adjusts his tie every two minutes. For the careless interviewer, these personal habits can become a mask that hides the real candidate. When impressions are damaged by such flak, the decision-making process breaks down. Interviewers are not so naive, of course, as to write down "smacks her lips" as a reason for rejecting the application. But they do err just as seriously in inventing reasons that supposedly justify a conclusion based on bias. Those false reasons are the ones called up in legal suits and often successfully refuted, at great expense to the company.

The Nettlesome Comment
Especially on stressful days, we each have "triggers" that can inadvertently be tripped by a candidate. It can be a wholly innocent remark: Q. "Were you able to find parking?" A. "Finally, but I had to drive around for twenty minutes. Is it like that every morning?" An overly sensitive interviewer could bristle at this remark, thinking "this guy's a complainer." Resist drawing conclusions based on a single comment. Wait to see if such comments form a trend in the person's expression or behavior.

The Kiss of Death

Often a candidate comes trailing clouds of glory or gore. In either case, discount the "hype" and look to the person and his or her qualifications. The kiss of death can come from a colleague: "I spoke briefly with Simmons—you won't be impressed." Just as often the comment can come from your secretary: "I think you'll like Kay Evans. She's very sweet." (You dislike sweet. In fact, you dislike your secretary. Her compliment of Kay Evans comes as the kiss of death.) Perhaps the most insidious form of influence comes from friends and superiors. We all want social approval and the boss's blessing. It's difficult, then, to ignore friends' and superiors' impressions long enough to form our own. But as interviewers, that's precisely our job.

The Look You Hate

Maybe it's the Annie Hall look or the Poindexter bow tie or the Miami Vice sports coat. We all have a look we just don't like. Usually it recalls for us a person from the past. But remember—that repugnant person is not sitting before us in the interview. The clothes do not make the person.

As Judge, the interviewer must resist other temptations to play God. One of the most common is the "Name that Tune" boast—"I can spot a poor candidate in ten seconds." Especially when interviewers talk among themselves in the company, this claim can take on the glamour of a macho challenge: "Let's see how fast we can 'process' these candidates." Skilled interviewers learn to resist their temptation to rush judgment.

The Judge at Work

Q. You've told me about your sales experience. How do you feel about cold calling?

A. (hesitates) I've done some. It isn't particularly hard.

Q. (gathers more input) You like it?

A. Well, no one likes cold calling. But there are times when it has to be done. I don't have problems with it.

Q. (tests tentative judgment) It's hard on the ego to be turned down by people you don't know?

A. It sure is. But, as I said, I can do it. I've done it before.

Judgement is finally based on the cumulative attitudes of hesitance and resistance expressed by the candidate.

THE PROFESSOR

Up to a third of selection interviews and even more of other forms of interviews are informational in nature. Candidates want to hear about the company, an employee requires a technical briefing, or a client needs product information. In all these cases, the interviewer plays Professor—with all the dangers traditionally associated with the profession.

Face it. Professors carry the reputation of being pompous, boring, and detached from "real life." George Bernard Shaw captured that sentiment well: "Those who can't do, teach."

In putting on the Professor hat for a few minutes in an interview, avoid the faux pas often associated with these wordmongers.

Don't Lecture—Converse
Even when delivering information in a one-way flow, do so in a conversational voice. Let your own feelings for your material add spontaneity and enthusiasm to your words.

Go for What Matters
Especially if you see signs of boredom, go straight for what matters most to your listener. Headline your key points in obvious ways: "Here's what it all adds up to, this is the key point, here's the bottom line."

Mix Your Media
We all liked the professor who took time to prepare good handouts, brought in slides, or showed an occasional film. He or she knew that spoken words, no matter how eloquent, fly by once and are gone. Interviewers can magnify the influence of their words and prevent boredom by having at hand brochures, fact sheets, and other supportive materials.

Professors, sad to say, often have a love affair with their own schtick. They light up at the opportunity to hold forth. They talk too much.

As an interviewer, don't. Watch your listener's eyes, posture, and physical shifting for signs of boredom and inattention.

The Professor at Work

> Q. Let me tell you a bit about the history of the company. It was founded in 1968 by Allen Dwight, an electrical engineer with a patent on the 3868 microprocessor. Our first customers were appliance and automobile manufacturers. But the real growth came in 1972 when we won a contract for computer parts on the Trident prototype. (notices a glaze settling over listener's eyes) Are you familiar with parallel-processing chips?
>
> A. Uh, yes. We worked with parallel-processing architecture in my computer systems design classes.
>
> Q. That was a big breakthrough for the company. You may not have realized that, as early as 1975, this company was doing development work for the government on parallel processors.

(The dialogue continues, with the interviewer making an effort to relate the company history to the listener's experiences and interests.)

The poet William Blake called professors "horses of instruction." As an interviewer, keep the phrase in mind the next time you're tempted to break into a long verbal dissertation. An executive at Goodyear Rubber warned his interviewers, "The longer the spoke, the greater the tire."

THE PRIEST

Especially in counseling interviews, the interviewer often plays the part of priest. He or she hears confessions of "sins," provides words of wisdom, and sometimes closes the interview with encouragement not unlike a blessing. The role of confidant can occur at times other than the counseling interview, of course. Job candidates can break suddenly into very personal information. In exit interviews, you may open the door to hearing truly desperate human dilemmas.

Wearing the robes of the Priest can be an uncomfortable experience for many interviewers. In their own lives, they draw a firm line between subjects appropriate for discussion at work and subjects reserved for private life. They expect others to do the same.

But others won't cooperate. At a disciplinary interview, Tom Lester breaks into tears over an alcohol habit he's been hiding for years. At an exit interview, Cindy Parker reveals improper sexual advances by her boss.

These moments call for special wisdom and humanity on the part of the interviewer. Guidelines vary according to the circumstances, but these may be helpful.

Don't Play Psychiatrist

Well-intentioned interviewers, especially when they feel deeply for the suffering of another person, sometimes take on more than they—or the company—is prepared to handle. Recognize that many employee dilemmas, including depression, drug dependency, alcoholism, and marital problems, require long-term professional help. Often the best help you can provide as a sympathetic counselor within the company is to make an employee aware of professional services he or she can afford.

Don't Bend the Rules Until They Break

All companies bend regulations to meet exceptional human needs. But interviewers should not ignore company priorities and policies in an effort to smooth the way for troubled employees. A major Ohio-based insurance company had to face this problem in a specific way. One interviewer in charge of midcareer counseling took it upon himself to play social worker for every human problem he encountered. On behalf of employees missing too much work he wrote indignant letters to management, accusing it of "insensitivity" to the employees' "personal problems." He intervened in raise determinations for low-performing employees by reciting a litany of "special circumstances." The end result was inevitable: management gave him a choice to stick to his job description or seek other employment. He chose the latter.

This is not to argue for cold disregard on the part of interviewer/counselors. It is to assert the important role of policies and procedures in dealing with human problems. In an effort to be fair to all employees, companies have to resist the temptation to be all things to all people. Interviewers should make themselves aware of company policies, precedents, and guidelines in order to find solutions that help the individual without crippling the business.

The Priest at Work

> Q. You began by saying that you and Jack have problems working together. What's going on?
>
> A. I used to blame him—his rough manner, his disorganized approach to management, his general sense of panic. But lately I've taken a hard look at myself. My anger.
>
> Q. (trying to understand) Your anger?
>
> A. I walk around like a time bomb some days—I really feel like I could explode. I guess a lot of it comes from home. My wife and I fight a lot, to put it mildly. And our kid is hanging out with a punk crowd that really scares me. Anyway, that plus Jack's antics are almost too much for me some days.
>
> Q. (wisely avoiding the role of psychologist or family counselor) I'm sorry to hear about the problems. Did you know your health plan here pays for professional counseling services?
>
> A. (interested) No, but I sure could use it.
>
> Q. Let me get the number for you to call. We both want to do whatever we can to solve this work problem.

Notice in this dialogue that the interviewer knew when not to pry more deeply. By asking in-depth questions about the employee's anger and its roots in marital and parental frustration, the interviewer would have been taking on the role of therapist—not what the company intended at all. Knowing how and when to guide troubled employees to professional help can be much more valuable in business circumstances than a misguided effort to play psychologist.

THE SALESPERSON

Finally, the company often sends interviewers into client, negotiation, telephone, and briefing interviews as salespersons. In this role, the interviewer is supposed to guide the flow of topics and conversations to specific ends: selling attitudes, ideas, products or services.

Selling, like courtship, is a relationship more than a one-way activity. No salesperson can claim (though many do) that "I sold it, but he just didn't buy it." The act of selling includes the act of buying.

In planning for sales actions, therefore, an interviewer should think beyond the "pitch" to building the sales relationship. Four components are especially important in that relationship.

Hearing What the Client Wants

It's a humbling but necessary prerequisite to effective selling to admit that the client may have something worth hearing. Partly as a defense against possible rejection and partly to maintain confidence, many salespersons create a psychological "script" for how the session with the client will proceed. Recipes for "how-to-sell-anything-to-anybody" encourage this kind of scripting.

While planning is important, remember that you have a coauthor helping you to create the interview: the client. Don't leave him or her out of the process, or plan so tightly for your own lines that you push aside anything he or she might offer.

Listen, first, for what the client wants or needs. Explore problems he or she faces because of those needs. Understand as deeply as possible the reasons why the client hasn't solved those problems. The route you eventually take toward your "solution" (i.e. what you're selling) will depend directly on how clearly you've understood the client's problem.

Turning Wants into Needs

A vastly successful California auto dealer put it this way: "People feel guilty over things they merely *want*. But they don't feel guilty having things they *need*." A salesperson's task, therefore, is to show the client how necessary certain ideas, services, or products are to him or her.

A client, for example, may want more highly trained secretaries so that documents don't leave the company flawed with grammatical and spelling errors. In an interview context, a salesperson can demonstrate how company profits depend directly on company image, and how image is affected by sloppy documents. What the client began by wanting now becomes something he or she needs. The effort and expense necessary to meet the need now seem less momentous—"We owe it to the company to protect its image."

Selling "on the Merits," Not on Special Pleading

One of the cruellest ironies of sales is that those who don't need clients must drive them off in droves, while those desperate for a sale can't find a buyer within miles.

Why? Because secure, successful salespeople give the impression they're working for the client's interests, not their own. "If I do a good job for you," they say in effect, "I know I'll be compensated fairly." By contrast, a struggling salesperson has that gleam of self-interest in the eye: "I need this sale so badly. Please don't say no."

Vacuums may be sold door-to-door by desperate young men and women working their way through college. But most things aren't. If clients sense self-seeking on the part of the salesperson, they clam up. They're consciously or subconsciously afraid of giving away feelings or information that can be used to maneuver them into action they may not want to take.

A secure salesperson, however, makes every effort to put the client at ease. The issue of whether or not the salesperson needs the sale never comes up. The focus, instead, is on the client's interest. In this sales environment, clients loosen up and, in telling their hopes and fears, go a long way toward selling themselves.

The Salesperson at Work

Q. You mentioned parking problems at your old office site.

A. A real mess. We finally had to hire an attendant to keep cars moving. I'd like to avoid that kind of problem if we can.

Q. It's important to. One of your biggest expenses is employee turnover, and the parking problem surely contributes to that expense.

A. Well, it's not the main reason people quit, but it gets mentioned pretty often in exit interviews as a big problem for employees.

Q. In choosing a new site, we need to solve that problem.

A. So add it to our priorities list—a site with adequate parking for 200 cars.

(The salesperson, in this exploratory interview, converts what the client wants into what the client needs.)

Each hat an interviewer wears carries with it opportunities, responsibilities, and liabilities. Switching from hat to hat, as all interviewers must, takes good verbal reflexes, creativity, and a good measure of common sense.

CHAPTER 3

YOUR ATTITUDES
FOR INTERVIEWING

For an interviewer eager to get on with it, to learn precisely what to do in certain situations, these preliminary chapters may at first seem too general. Where are the recipes, the sample questions to use, the do's and don'ts?

They're coming aplenty in the later sections. But let me make a plea that you don't skip over Chapters 3 through 6. Here's why.

Interviewing is a complex human activity that pits all that you are against all that the interviewee is. Your ego, your dignity, your sense of humor, your smarts, your verbal abilities, your ethics, and much more are on the line in an interview.

No simple recipe fits your complexity. To grow as an interviewer, to understand more deeply what you're up to and up against, think through the pages of chapters 3 through 6. Every paragraph and page deals with attitudes and skills that make for effective interviewing. These matters are the hub of the wheel. All interview techniques radiate from them.

BUILDING RAPPORT

In a recent survey, I asked midlevel managers active in interviewing to define rapport. More than 80 percent associated the word with some aspect of friendliness: "a friendly spirit between interviewer and interviewee," "cheerfulness on the part of both parties," "a general level of comfort and relaxation in the interview."

That's Valium, not rapport. If we understand what rapport really is, we can recognize when it's present and when it isn't. We can also learn to create it.

Rapport comes directly from a French verb meaning "to bring back." Bring back to what? In an interview, rapport exists when both parties are continually brought back to the moment at hand (what psychologists call "the now"). Neither party goes off on a self-indulgent tangent, ignoring looks of confusion and frustration. Neither party sits silent and stubborn, refusing to respond to the stimulus of conversation. In a phrase, they are "in touch."

Does rapport, therefore, have to be friendly? Not at all. Two parties struggling through a painful disciplinary interview can be in profound rapport with one another. The managers cited above mistook rapport for friendliness simply because it is in friendship that we most often experience true rapport.

When we're together with a close friend, we are aware, minute by minute, of subtle shifts in feeling, shadings of intonation, physical expressions of emotion, and all that's said between the lines. In common parlance, friends "care" for one another. They don't ignore or overlook the many communication signals passing from one person to the other. (Admittedly, this close attention to signals from our friends isn't always conscious, as it might be for a social scientist. In a comfortable way, friends simply know that there is a special awareness and mutual interest between them, even when not called to consciousness.)

Now the key question for interviewers: do you want to have this rapport with total strangers in an interview situation? Might it not be better to avoid rapport, keeping the interview "businesslike"?

Interviews without rapport are possible (in fact, they take place by the thousands every day). But how much they miss! Lacking rapport, interviewers

Miss or Misinterpret Nonverbal Signals
The lack of eye contact and fidgeting are seen, but not understood in relation to what caused or accompanied them.

Fail to Communicate the Company's Sincere Interest in the Interviewee
Failure to "connect" works both ways. If the interviewer feels out of touch and somewhat distanced from the concerns of the interviewee, those same feelings are probably felt by the interviewee toward both the interviewer and the company.

Lose Opportunities for Meaningful Questions
Lacking rapport, an interview becomes a ritual of standard questions and predictable answers. The whole process could take place more efficiently and less expensively by mail.

ADJUSTING YOUR EXPECTATIONS

Because they misunderstand the nature of rapport, many beginning interviewers expect to "click" with each interviewee who walks through the door. (By "click" they mean feel an immediate chemistry of mutual interest and mutual good humor–in short, a liking for one another.) If that bond isn't established in the first minute or two of chat, these interviewers tend to blame the interviewee: "somewhat impersonal," "shy," "withdrawn," "aloof," "too earnest," "lacks personality."

Don't expect to feel immediate liking for each interviewee — you're not Will Rogers. And don't blame the candidate or yourself for this response. It's perfectly natural to withhold affection from strangers until we feel a sincere surge of liking within. That can take a matter of hours, days, or it may never happen at all. The fact is that, as interviewers, we can't fake affection for long without feeling cheap and insincere. We shouldn't try.

Expect, instead, to find interest in each person you interview. That interest can extend to the way he or she looks, speaks, thinks, responds to questions, laughs, and all the other aspects of human interaction. Rapport, remember, is nothing more or less than staying with the moment—what's happening right now in the emerging relationship. Your interest, moment by moment, is a sure way to establish and maintain such rapport.

The interviewee feels your interest and responds in kind. Will he or she be disappointed that you haven't gone out of your way to show liking in addition to interest? Usually not, at least for emotionally mature candidates (the kind you want to hire!). There is considerable security and freedom in a business environment that can detach personal preferences and tastes from professional purposes. Candidates may well feel relief that "liking" isn't the primary standard by which they are being judged.

STEPS TO RAPPORT

Granted, rapport can pay important dividends in the interviewing process. But how is it achieved?

Step One. Break the Ice

At the beginning of any social relationship, someone must take the risk of the first move. Especially when you're playing host for interviews at your location, that first move is yours. It should involve some degree of effort. If the candidate is waiting in your foyer, go out to get him or her. If your secretary brings the candidate to your office, step out from behind your desk and move forward to shake hands. These nonverbal gestures go a long way toward saying "I care about this interview."

Step Two. Open with Nonthreatening Topics

Your first goal, in opening conversation, is to indicate (without wearing your heart on your sleeve) that you're pleasant, personable, and fair. Your second goal—one often forgotten by interviewers—is to give the interviewee a chance to show the same things.

Under the influence of nerves, the candidate's defenses are up at the beginning of the interview. You can lower those defenses so communication can begin to take place. The technique involves bringing up "no harm, no foul" topics. The interviewee should feel that the real interview hasn't yet begun—that he or she can chat freely without being judged. Therefore, you'll want to choose topics that will arouse interest and response on the part of the interviewee. Here are some traditional openers.

> *the weather* (believe it or not, this old standby still works)
>
> *interviewee's convenience or comfort* (parking, hotel, traffic, etc.)
>
> *first impressions* (of corporate offices, city, region)
>
> *reference to college* (including sports teams, alumni, professors, programs)
>
> *mutual acquaintances*

Steer clear of opening remarks intended as humorous but also open to interpretation as criticism. One interviewer, for example, greeted women candidates with "I see you have your power suit on—I'd better watch out!" The remark was innocent, but many interviewees took it as a slanting blow against their choice of clothes.

Also avoid self-centered topics such as current hassles around the office, bizarre or problematic personalities on the staff, and inhouse news. These topics are easy for you to talk about, but leave the interviewee with nothing to say. As mentioned above, an important goal of your opening remarks is to give the interviewee a chance to come out of his or her shell. The interviewee can't be expected to talk with enthusiasm or knowledge about plumbing failures in the executive men's room.

Finally, exercise caution in beginning with "jeopardy" questions. One Toledo executive made it a regular habit to steer interviewees immediately to a large modernistic painting behind his desk. "What do you think of it?" was his first question. The candidate, understandably nervous, is put in a difficult position: "Is this a test? If so, what does it have to do with the job? Should I be polite—it's his office, after all. Should I be blunt? Maybe that's what he expects." The result of such quandaries is a tongue-tied candidate, off to a bad start in the interview. (Once rapport has been established, of course, there is an important place for these sorts of questions.)

PHYSICAL RAPPORT

The bond you establish with the interviewee goes beyond the words you say. Your firm handshake, reassuring facial expression, natural eye contact, dress, and posture send important messages. So powerful are these messages, in fact, that they prove more creditable than words themselves when the two are in conflict. If your nonverbal cues say, "I'm in a hurry and anxious to get this interview over with," no suave verbal assurances will persuade the interviewee otherwise.

An important aspect of physical rapport is the rapid ping-pong game of expressions we play in rapport relations. The candidate raises an eyebrow, you smile; the candidate hesitates, you lean forward; the candidate laughs, you sit back and laugh, too. The key here is not to think of yourself as a sequestered jury detached from the interview, but, instead, a participant who is largely responsible for creating the communication that takes place. Let yourself respond naturally and frequently, therefore, to cues sent by the interviewee.

USING AND ABUSING POWER

So far we have described the opening of the interview as a rather gracious social transaction in which you as "host" put the interviewee at ease as much as possible.

View that same scenario, however, through the eyes of the interviewee—Barbara, let's say. She's sees you robed in almost absolute power over her welfare and destiny (assuming, of course, that she "really wants this job.") What's more, she's on your turf with your minions surrounding her. On a power scale of one to ten, she ranks you as a ten plus and herself as a one minus. At no other time in your relationship will the power balance be seen in quite this extreme a way. If you hire Barbara, for example, she will have rights and recourses that limit your power over her and her career. But for now, you are the sole door to the kingdom.

Frankly, many bosses revel in that sensation of power. For some, it is the primary attraction in becoming a manager. They like the sense of importance showered on them by disenfranchised, powerless interviewees. These bosses like being tall hog at the trough.

And too often that yen on the part of management for being stroked ("O Thou Swell") destroys the interview process. The company misses out on good people and instead hires sycophants.

The abuse of power in interviews happens, often subtly, in three principle ways.

The Pucker Test
Early in the interview the power-crazed (and often insecure) manager will invent a test of the candidate's willingness to kiss up. If the candidate passes the test, the ground rules for the Big Me-Little You relationship have been established and the interview can proceed. If the candidate fails the test, the interview turns perfunctory and often sarcastic.

Q. I'm going to hold my calls–don't mind all these red lights lighting up on the phone.

A. (candidate glances at phone)

Q. (being more obvious) I probably get 20 calls an hour.

A. (candidate nods)

Q. (lays it on with a trowel) But you know what they say: "If you can't stand the heat, stay out of the kitchen."

A. (finally catches on) You keep a lot of fishing lines in the water. It must be a real challenge to know what all your people are up to.

The boss accepts this compliment and goes on to bluster a bit about how important it is to have a manager who really knows operations from the ground up.

The Whipping of the Slaves

A second abuse of power in interviews is what most secretaries know as "interview insults." To show his or her authority, the boss strikes out at a nearby employee: "Wanda, if I've told you once, I've told you a thousand times—make at least six copies of this candidate's resume!" The tone, the temper, the grimace all are intended to impress the candidate. The mood, of course, is never taken out on the interviewee directly. More often, the candidate is spoken to as a confidant who has observed the grievous injuries the boss has sustained: "Can you believe people like that? What an idiot!"

In this manipulative and often harmful way, the boss flexes his or her managerial muscle to the potential new hire. The intent is to impress and warn the candidate. The result, however, is often quite the reverse: both the candidates and the employees lose respect for a bozo who can manage only by anger.

The Company I Keep

A third common abuse of power in interviews is gross name dropping. It begins by an undue emphasis on titles. The boss makes a major point of his or her title as Acting Vice President in Charge of Western Sales—"and the Acting will soon be dropped." Then follows the frequent mention of the boss's closest associates, a coterie of executives who make all the real decisions. A series of introductions is often promised—"I'll get you in to meet the president of the company as soon as she returns from France. I asked the chief financial officer to ring me later this morning. You'll enjoy meeting him too." The introductions seldom happen.

Why does an otherwise able manager clutter the beginning of an interview with this elaborate facade? Because he or she is anxious to establish dominance from the beginning over the new kid on the block. The routine recalls the rooster's antics in maintaining the pecking order.

Aside from making managers look foolish, such trumpeting ruins interviews by forcing interviewees into insincere, ingratiating, self-debasing expressions. Faced with a manager bragging about his or her importance to the company, an interviewee has few choices in response other than to express admiration or a desire to imitate. And there's the rub: should the employee who admires the boss the most get the job? Of course not. But the abuse of power sets up the ground rules that make this selection criterion almost inevitable.

THE USES OF POWER

We're not suggesting that bosses perpetuate the false illusion that there is no chain of command, no pecking order within the company. Power is a reality. But to express it in an interview is an art. The key is to put power relations in proper perspective so as not to force less powerful people into insincere, unproductive, and dishonest positions.

In an interview, what's not said about the boss's prestige and power is more influential in a positive way than what's said. Take a hard look at your office, the interview site. Does it speak of an orderly, balanced, creative approach to managing projects and people? Are the perks of accomplishment evident in a tasteful way? Does the environment suggest an active form of success that doesn't rest on its laurels?

The interview experience (including its physical setting) tells the candidate a great deal about the company. Take as much time thinking through the physical messages your office or interview location sends as you do in preparing interview questions.

Your personnel staff and secretaries can also do much to assert your power without alienating or squelching the interviewee. What does the screening interviewer from your personnel office say about you as he or she walks the candidate to your office? What does your secretary say to the candidate during the five or ten minutes of waiting prior to an interview?

These people can prove extremely valuable in characterizing you for the candidate: "I think you'll like Ms. Garrington. She's been very successful with the company and was promoted last year to director of marketing." The expression can be natural, not speechy–part of the conversation that candidates need and want to hear prior to an interview. But those brief sentences do more to get an interview off on the right foot than an hour of the boss's self-aggrandisement.

The uses of power, then, should be devoted to one end: demonstrating to the interviewee that control and authority are exercised in an orderly, humane, and sensitive way within the company. Bosses should want their reputations to precede them for candidates. These newcomers will give more in the interview and get more positive impressions of the company when they respect the person, position, and accomplishments of the interviewer.

DIRECTIVE AND NONDIRECTIVE RELATIONS

Companies need to know that employees can follow orders and also act intelligently in the absence of specific orders. Resumes and applications don't divulge this information. The interview, therefore, is often the last and only occasion to decide whether the candidate is a wimp, a whacko, or a winner.

Directive relations in interviews are familiar, as in the following example:

Q. Tell me why you chose journalism as an undergraduate minor.
A. I thought it would be good to brush up my writing skills. Managers are doing more writing than ever.

The interviewer directs the candidate to a specific task, then judges how well the task is accomplished. Represented visually, the interviewer draws the boundary line, then asks the interviewee to color within the lines as neatly as possible.

The advantages of the directive approach to interviewing are many, accounting for its wide use (and, as we shall see, its overuse).

- Questions can be structured in advance based on job requirements.
- The interview flows smoothly, with few awkard "let-me-think" hesitations on the part of the interviewee.
- The information received is usually brief, to-the-point, and easy to record.
- Candidates can be compared more easily, since each has faced an identical set of questions and tasks.
- Interviewers can be trained more easily; they require less skill in making judgments, sophisticated discriminations, and logical inferences.
- Time allotments for interviews can be scheduled more accurately.

Examples of Directive Questions

"What courses from college were particularly valuable to you?"
"What was your GPA?"
"Did you work during college?"
"How would you characterize your personality?"
"Are you willing to travel as part of your job?"

Notice that each of these questions demands a content answer— a few sentences that can be boiled down (and written down) as a key word or two. If that word is right, you get the job. If not, "We appreciate your interest and will keep your materials on file."

NONDIRECTIVE QUESTIONS

Interviews are so filled with directive questions that we sometimes forget the alternative: questions and conversation that solicit not content responses but process responses. The difference is crucial. A content response is "the answer," with no attention to how the answer was arrived at. A process response, however, is evaluated by more complex standards: how the interviewee fielded the question, conceptualized the problem, arranged the argument, ordered examples and evidence, and drew conclusions. While content responses are a measurement of recall and broad judgments, process responses reveal habits of mind, qualities of thinking, and powers of conceptualization and organization.

Too many directive questions early in an interview establish a directive mindset on the part of the interviewee. He or she comes to look at the interviewer as a parent figure–the one who provides structure, order, organization. The interviewee simply tries to fit in with the established plan without introducing unexpected elements– like an original thought.

It is preferable, therefore, to use both directive and nondirective questions in appropriate balance throughout the interview. Each yields valuable insight into the candidate.

Examples of Nondirective Questions and Comments

"We hear and read a lot about ethics in business these days. Have you given business ethics much thought?"

"Our last sales manager disliked having to travel one week a month."

"I notice you've changed jobs about once a year." (pause)

Notice in these questions that it's impossible to color neatly within the lines. No lines are clearly drawn by the interviewer. The candidate must wrestle with the topic area, give it shape in keeping with his or her own insights, then express and support a point of view.

Here are two responses to the last question about changing jobs once a year. What could you conclude about processes of thought (not content) from the responses?

Q. I notice you've changed jobs about once a year.

Response 1. But in three of those cases it wasn't really my fault. I had jobs while I was still attending college and had to quit when my father was transferred to another state. Because of residency require- ments it made sense for me to go with my family rather than stick it out paying out-of-state tuition. In Nebraska, for example, out-of- state tuition was going to run me $4300 a year. I simply couldn't afford that. So even though my job record looks bad, there really were circumstances that explain most of the changes.

Response 2. As my skills in computer science developed, I found I had more and more to offer. In three cases there simply wasn't room to grow within the company. In the fourth, it was a matter of money.

I had a better offer just when I needed it most—my senior year in college. I'm interested in this company because you have a wide range of projects and exceptional expertise. It's the kind of place where I would want to stay because I could grow and also contribute.

Ignoring the content of the responses, what do you note in the habits of mind, the mental processes, at work in each case?

In Response 1, the knee-jerk reaction to an observation regarding job changes was to take it as negative criticism. Then follows a rambling defense, with unnecessary details such as the costs of out-of-state tuition in Nebraska. The candidate ignores the obvious interest of the interviewer—will you stay with this job?—and narrowly pursues self-justification and self-defense.

In Response 2, the candidate converts a potential criticism into an opportunity for salesmanship. After a straightforward explanation, the candidate turns to the interviewer's obvious intent in raising the issue. The reassurance offered is based on positive aspects of the company itself.

Nondirective questions suffer from a bad, but undeserved, reputation: people say they're impossible to record. Not so. If the interviewer understands what to look for, he or she can record many qualities of a candidate's thinking, based on responses to nondirective questions.

• Positive: "good problem definition," "logical," "sticks to the point," "sincere," "backs up argument well," "senses real intent of question," and so forth.
• Negative: "unnecessarily defensive," "wanders from topic," "illogical," "emotional, not rational," "no support for points," and so forth.

This kind of evidence can be of great importance in trying to find Mr. or Ms. Right, especially when the position involves skills more complex than shrink-wrapping widgets.

Interviewers establishing nondirective relations must prepare themselves for more "social ambiguity" in the interview process itself than they would experience in directive relations. Answers are more complex and less predictable when adults speak to adults rather than parents to children. Interviewees sometimes stare at the floor, thinking. Silences fall. Both parties struggle at times for the right words. And, for experienced nondirective interviewers, that's OK. In fact, it's preferable to a sole diet of glib, stimulus-response answers of the directive sort.

LOCATING AND CONTROLLING BIASES

Me, biased? Even the word conjures up beefy state militia barring the doors of Mississippi classrooms.

The fact is that we are each—including the author—a walking zoo of biases, presuppositions, assumptions, moods, and downright prejudices.

Let's get the obvious ones off our plate right away: we don't look down on people for their color (unless their hair is dyed in a primary color), their religion (unless it's something "weird," like Krishna or Rajneesh), their politics (as long as they're Republican, Democrat, or Independent), or sexual preference (as long as it doesn't show if they're homosexual). Our innocence even in these areas, it seems, is a bit tarnished.

We can keep bias out of our interviews (and our companies out of court) only by exercising self-control. Innocence isn't an option.

Which biases and prejudices in particular afflict the interview process? Here's a "Five Most Unwanted" list, to which you may want to add your own.

Judging a Candidate by Looks
A mountain of recent research demonstrates that tall, trim men and pretty, slim women fare better than their equally qualified, but shorter and homelier counterparts, when applying for jobs across industries.

Which "look" spells success for you? Preppy? Brooks Brothers? Ives St. Laurent? Greenwich Village? Beach Boys? The goal is not to change your preferences in dress (or weight or height, for that matter), but to face up to a danger. You may miss a gold mine of good people over the years if you leap to judgement based on dress. Define for yourself, therefore, your predisposition. Then control its influence in your decision making.

Basing Decisions on Accent
We're almost past the day, thank God, when blacks, Orientals, Chicanos, and others simply didn't have a chance in many hiring situations. They do have a chance now—but with a catch. They have to speak English about as well as Dan Rather. No matter that they speak four languages and read seven. We're still obsessed with accent, even when a candidate's speech is perfectly understandable. We're afraid what the accent may suggest to "others" (always uniden-

tified) about the company's standards and image. A British accent, of course, would be lovely. Irish will do. Australian a bit less so. Cantonese only in some circumstances. And Indian, Cuban, Mexican, Puerto Rican? Forget it!

Face two facts: Overcoming an accent is the work of a lifetime, not a month or two. Highly skilled individuals who are non-native speakers will not sound like Dan Rather overnight. Second, clear speakers with accents do not impede business or tarnish images. That's Regency Club thinking that passed into a coma long ago. Bilingual managers, in fact, are in great demand throughout the country.

Every accent, like an aroma, quickly takes us to memories and locations from our past. These mind trips are quite beyond our conscious control—but not beyond our management. Here's an example. A young man comes in for an interview. He's impeccably dressed and bears an admirable resume. His accent, though—ouch! It's Spanish. You can understand every word he says, but it sounds so . . . so Mexican. And there you are—riding the subway as a 10-year-old, looking out of spray-painted windows at a Mexican gang "rumbling" in the metro station. All the lousy memories flood back along with racial jokes and stereotypes.

Grab hold. The Mexican gang isn't sitting in front of you. Robert Velasquez *is*, GPA 3.7 from Wharton. Learn to face up to the difference betwen fact and phastasm.

The issue, then, in resolving the accent question is not whether the candidate's speech reveals ethnicity—of course it does. (Your accent and mine, too, speak volumes about our backgrounds.) The issue is simply clarity. Can the man or woman be understood for business purposes? If so, accent need not be considered.

Drawing Conclusions from Pedigree

The interview process is often onerous. Short cuts are tempting. One that backfires regularly—and expensively—for companies is the "pedigree myth" in its various forms. Some companies, after hiring three good workers from Local State University, make up their minds: "Local State produces the kind of candidates we want. Don't give others serious c.nsideration."

Other interviewers focus on a particular major. Have you taken at least three computer courses of whatever kind? You're in. Are you a finance major with an econ minor? Just what we're looking for.

Such rigid insistence on a particular configuration of undergraduate experiences overrates academia's abilities and underrates the company's internal training alternatives. Virtually all companies discover that a certain amount of on-the-job education is necessary, no matter how high the student's GPA or prestigious the college. In a matter of weeks companies can usually bring bright new hires up to speed even if they lack one or more of the "must have" courses or experiences in the job description.

In short, plan job descriptions to indicate desirable backgrounds. But don't let job descriptions and job ads limit your ability to attract and hire the right person because of unnecessarily rigid specifications.

Being Blinded by the Halo

Some candidates will remind you ever so much of that legendary employee—yourself. They may look like you at an earlier stage in your career, or have the same sensitive, energetic spirit. By coincidence they may like the same sports you do, or hold membership in the same church or civic organization.

"There's just something I like about the person," you reflect after the interview. Suddenly the candidate's mediocre transcript and so-so work experiences seem to glow in a way they hadn't before, all thanks to the halo effect.

Alan Pedersen, president of Healthcare Affiliates, Inc. saw this problem among his company's interviewers. "They weren't asking the right questions," he say. "They used the 'halo effect.' If they saw themselves in the person, someone who dresses nicely and has a good personality, they'd hire. They weren't placing enough emphasis on the candidate's prior work history,"

Guard against this distortion by reminding yourself, hard though it may be at times, to exert fair and equal evaluative energy on each candidate. When, in interviewing a candidate, the bell of self-recognition goes off, let it be your signal to exercise professional, evenhanded judgment, not special treatment.

Selecting by Time, Not Qualifications

As most of us discover after cross-country flights, we do have "bio-clocks" that affect our energy levels, moods, and general comfort.

Such bio-clocks operate to our disadvantage in many interview situations.

Take the following scenario: Candidate A sees you for a 9 A.M. Monday interview. The coffee tastes awful this morning. You're groggy from a late Sunday night. You've had words with your spouse shortly before coming to work. Besides, you're just not a "morning person." Candidate B arrives for a 1:30 P.M. interview. You're cheery after a lunch with work pals. You've made up with your spouse. You're "in gear" again.

No matter what their relative qualifications, which candidate is more likely to get your favorable nod? You guessed—the one in sync with your internal bio-clock.

To guard against selection by time, not qualification, be as objective as possible about your mood and mental acuity prior to meeting the interviewee. By facing up to your potential liabilities as an interviewer, you can work hard to ask good questions, listen well, and respond carefully and sensitively. If you doubt your ability on a particular day to pull back from the black hole of moods, bring a colleague in to observe the interview. Talk through your reactions with your coworker afterwards as a way of evaluating the fairness of your judgments.

Interviewers have different "danger zones," of course, during the day. Some are particularly hard on candidates at the end of the day. Others are particularly cranky just before meals, or lethargic and inattentive immediately after meals. As an empirical check on the effect of mood, interviewers should keep track over a period of months of the time slots when "yes, hire!" interviews took place. If they all group toward one period of the day or week, with unsuccessful candidates falling in other periods, there is a good prima facie case for distortion based on the bio-clock of the interviewer.

Socrates urged "Know thyself." All our professional and personal actions radiate from that nervecenter of selfhood. If the hub of our deepest assumptions and predispositions is unknown to us, the surrounding structure and meaning of our actions will be haphazard and inconsistent. As a step in refining your own self-knowledge, consult Box 3–1. Note that there is no perfect score possible—none of us is in the running for sainthood. But each question can help you raise questions about and find answers for areas of bias and prejudice. The results can be especially helpful if two or more interviewers discuss their respective choices together.

Box 3–1
Checklist for Locating and Controlling Bias

The purpose of this worksheet is to bring potentially discriminatory prejudices to the level of consciousness, where they can be dealt with rationally. The worksheet is best used immediately after an interview is concluded, but before interview results are recorded. Read each question, then attempt to answer it aloud. The exercise should take no more than a few minutes—time well-spent if it helps the interviewer avoid errors in judgment.

The Candidate's Appearance and Behavior

- Whom does the candidate remind me of? (Be aware that the candidate is not that person.)
- How do I feel about the candidate's style of dress? (Be aware that your attitudes toward dress probably have little to do with job qualifications.)
- How do I feel about the candidate's size, weight, skin color, and other physical characteristics? (Be aware that successful employees come in all sizes, shapes, and colors.)

The Candidate's Background

- What assumptions have I made based on the region from which the candidate came? (Be aware that your attitudes toward the candidate's hometown should not color your view of the person.)
- How do I feel about the college or university attended by the candidate? (Be aware that college reputations have little to do with the candidate's individual qualities.)
- What assumptions have I made based on the candidate's job history? (Be aware that excellent employees often do not have ideal job histories, as measured by job titles and company prestige.)

The Interview Situation

- How do I as an interviewer feel today? (Be aware that moods, weariness, and other physical and emotional feelings can influence your judgment.)
- In what ways is my attitude toward the candidate affected by the physical setting, time, schedule, surrounding activities, other commitments, and so forth? (Be aware that your attitudes toward the time and place of the interview can be projected onto the candidate.)

Other Areas of Potential Bias

- What do others in the company expect me to conclude about this candidate?
- How does the company usually deal with this kind of candidate?
- How does the fairness or unfairness of my own workload influence my attitudes toward this interview?
- How do present situations in my personal life affect my feelings toward the candidate?

CHAPTER 4

VERBAL TECHNIQUES
FOR INTERVIEWING

"I got the clear impression that he didn't like me," said Virginia R. as she left an interview for an accounting position with a southern California aerospace company. "It wasn't so much what he said as the way he said it."

The interviewer, Franklin E., told the other side of the story. "She was bright and had good background skills, but seemed timid and distant. I didn't think she would fit in with the accounting group."

In the fast ping-pong game of interviewing, it's difficult to say who makes the first bad serve. But one thing's for sure: once the ball begins to spin out of control, both players are put off their game.

The ways in which words are said can drastically affect our perceptions and actions. Call it the "restaurant effect." We've all been there: A waiter asks what we want to eat, but in the tone, volume, and pace we hear another message—"I'm busy, Mac. Give me your order and be quick about it." That false start can influence how we feel about the food we eventually receive and about the restaurant itself. (A Boston communications firm, incidentally, does seminars for waiters who do "everything right" but still get low tips. The emphasis, not surprisingly, is on tone of voice and personal manner.)

THE COMPONENTS OF VERBAL ACTION

Some interviewers think of the interview process as inactivity—except for occasional gestures, bodily movements, and facial expressions, they hardly move. Yet action in the truest sense ("change of position or status") is taking place—verbally. Your words and the way you say them are the movers and pushers, for better or for worse.

As suggested in Figure 4–1, the interviewer's verbal arsenal can be divided into seven categories. From greatest to least in influence, they are tone, volume, pace, emphasis, pauses, articulation, and pitch.

TONE

By the time we're three years old we know how to recognize and interpret the tone of communications addressed to us: "Not now, Billy!" means Mom or Dad is close to the edge of anger. "Maybe in a little while," said in a surrendering tone, means we're close to getting our wishes, with just a bit more whining. By the time we're five or six, we've mastered much of the art of tone ourselves. We specialize in the pout, the taunt, the innocent alibi, the ultimatum— and all the other ways the words are set apart from their specific content.

The art of tone is progressively refined as we mature. By the time we've entered our professional lives we can shade our words with implied threat, suggested guilt, humor, sarcasm, intimacy, despair, and a wide range of other feelings and intentions.

Above all, we've mastered the "inner-outer" game in the tone we use. On the one hand, we choose a tone that tells something about how we feel on the inside about the words we're saying. When we reveal those feelings through our tone and other means, the listener feels we're sincere—that is, our feelings square with the content of the words we're saying and the actions we're taking.

FIGURE 4–1
Verbal Components

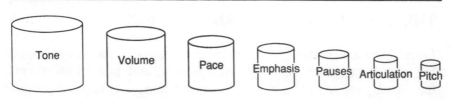

On the other hand, however, we can choose a tone that is directed outward, not inward, to accomplish a particular purpose. This tone may or may not reveal our sincere feelings; its real intent is to produce certain responses within the listener. We choose an angry tone, perhaps, not because we're truly angry but because we want to intimidate the listener. We choose a tough, brusque tone in negotiations as a way of seeing what concessions the other party is willing to make.

Our tone is manipulative when it differs from what we, in fact, really feel. Skilled interviewers use both sincerity and manipulation in tone in their efforts to explore the potential of the interview.

Time out: is it ethical to "fake" feelings in your tone of voice to produce certain responses or reactions on the part of the interviewee? Emphatically yes. The interviewer's implied ethical contract with the interviewee can be stated simply: "I will give you a clear, truthful picture of what the company needs and offers; I will create ample opportunities for you to reveal what you need and offer; I will judge you fairly."

The process of creating opportunities for self-revelation by the candidate of course often involves a "what if" world, both in content and tone. "What if you were asked to supervise several other employees, all much more experienced than yourself?" Here the content is hypothetical, and the candidate's response can be valuable in measuring his or her usefulness to the company. "I understand what you're saying, but I strongly disagree!" (said with energy). Here the tone is hypothetical—the interviewer is consciously creating a moment of stress—and the way the interviewee responds to such stress can again provide valuable information for the company.

In short, interviewers like actors have the license—in fact, the obligation—to draw upon a wide range of verbal techniques in a good cause; the creation of opportunities for in-depth self-revelation on the part of the interviewee.

Varieties of Tone

Like personality itself, tone can take on innumerable shadings and characteristics. Interviewers have traditionally relied on six basic tone patterns, however, to evoke and explore the intellect and emotions of the candidate.

1. The Suspicious Tone

"You say you did very well in your major courses. Would your professors vouch for that?" (said with a strong insinuation of doubt). How does an interviewee respond when his or her assertions are called into question? With a flare of temper? With a confession? With a stand-off?—"I don't know. Why don't you call them?"

These reactions can tell you much about a candidate's integrity, maturity, ability to deal constructively with criticism, and ability to work with people.

The suspicious tone must be used with discretion. Too much suspicion will seem a flagrant challenge to the candidate's integrity, producing indignation and a breakdown in communication. But in lesser and occasional doses, an inquiring, suspicious tone can be a useful scalpel in cutting through surface proprieties to the candidate's instinctive emotional reactions.

Sample Questions Using the Suspicious Tone

"What real supervisory duties did you perform as 'head of inventory staff' during your summer at XYZ Corporation?"

"You've attributed many of your lower grades to personality problems with professors. Don't these sorts of problems occur a bit frequently?"

"Why did you quit your last position after only two months on the job?"

Note that these questions could be said in many ways, including in a sincere, open tone. The point is that each tone an interviewer chooses to use opens windows to certain aspects of the candidate's nature and potential. The suspicious tone is one among many choices.

2. The Jovial Tone

"Ha! Your fraternity experience sounded a lot like mine. Did you feel it gave you an edge getting through your classes?"

The jovial tone creates a mood of trust, approval, and acceptance. In that environment, many candidates will give away information they might withhold from a more distanced interviewer. In the case above, a candidate responded with the laugh-a-minute story of fraternity high jinks, including purloined tests and purchased term papers. The company needed to measure the ethics of the candidate, and this unwitting confession helped provide data for that measurement.

Has the interviewer "tricked" the candidate into revealing more than he or she should have? No. Wrongful deception is present only if the interviewer entraps the candidate by assurance that information 'won't be used against you' or by false modeling ("We all cheated in college. Did you, too?"). If the interviewer is simply creating a nonthreatening environment for conversation, no trickery is involved. The candidate may speak in ways that do not serve his or her interest, but the interviewer has not "set up" the interviewee for such revelations.

Sample Questions Using the Jovial Tone

"I can tell you're really into physical fitness and the outdoor life. How do you find time to work?"

"As you say, you've had your share of 'weird' bosses in the past jobs. What are some early signs to you that the boss is, in your word, 'weird'?"

"I guess we all like to have friends at work. What would you do if someone didn't fit into the big, happy family?"

3. The Impatient Tone

"We all run on a fast track at this company. As briefly as possible, tell me how you handle deadlines and time stress."

Especially for candidates who come to the interview with prepared speeches to recite, an impatient tone and short, blunt questions can throw them off their game plan—and reveal much about their ability to scramble under pressure. Employees at all levels, after all, need the flexibility to cope with unexpected circumstances and unforeseen deadlines.

In using an impatient tone, the interviewer need not sound disapproving or hostile, but simply in a hurry for an answer that makes sense. Physicians have honed the impatient question to an art: when a patient begins a long, rambling narrative, the physician politely but curtly cuts in with a specific question. Interviewers can use this tone, including interruptions as necessary, to test the candidate's ability to think on his or her feet.

Sample Questions Using the Impatient Tone

"I've read your transcript. Sum up for me in a few words what you got from a business education."

"There are a thousand things we could talk about, but I don't have time. What's special about you that makes you right for this job?"

"I've only got six minutes left before we bring in the next candidate. What do you think we should cover in the time that's left?"

4. The Intimate Tone

"Just between you and me, this company is turning into a real United Nations. Have you ever worked side by side with minorities?"

Notice that this question is not said with a derogatory tone, which might predispose the candidate's response. Rather, it is said in an intimate, "just-the-two-of-us, person-to-person" tone.

What candidates offer freely in this intimate environment can differ substantially from what they answer to more bald questions ("How do you relate to members of other ethnic groups?"). In the case of the intimate inquiry above, a candidate might shrug off the question with "I did my job and they did theirs—we left each other alone" and thereby tell volumes about attitudes and predispositions.

The intimate tone, like the jovial tone, should not be used to entrap the candidate by inviting concurrence with the interviewer's own attitudes. Instead, the intimate tone simply asserts, "I'm being informal and unguarded in my question. I want you to do the same in your answer."

Sample Questions Using the Intimate Tone

"College courses always have fancy titles. But which ones really gave you something you could use?"

"You've had the official tour and met all the big shots around here. But, bottom line, what are your feelings about the work environment?"

"I guess everyone has certain doubts or anxieties going into a new position. What are some of the things you're unsure about when you think about this job?"

5. *The Neutral Tone*

"Have you ever been supervised by a member of the opposite sex? Tell me about your experience." (said in a tone that does not reveal the interviewer's attitude)

Ironically, the neutral tone is among the hardest to perfect as an interviewer. Psychologist Carl Rogers points out that to inquire about another person's attitudes without a hint of judgment is "a rare experience in this world, and a precious one." The neutral tone should not reflect malaise, boredom, or lack of interest. Nor should it sound robot-like and sterile.

Instead, the neutral tone is delivered evenly, without suggestion of the interviewer's own emotional predispositions. If, for example, the question above were asked with a big sigh, the candidate might conclude that the company applies sexual stereotypes to the promotion process. When the question is delivered neutrally, the candidate can make no such assumptions. His or her answer, uninfluenced by the interviewer's stance, can be valuable data for the selection process.

Ordinary conversations are hardly ever neutral in tone. For this reason, many interviewers rarely use the neutral tone for questions, trying to keep the interview "lively." Without sacrificing this energetic give-and-take, interviewers should recognize, nevertheless, that an interview is more than a conversation. The goals of an interview go far beyond the goals of an ordinary conversation, and for that reason the range of tones used in an interview usually exceeds those found in conversation.

Sample Questions Using the Neutral Tone

"You've worked for two of our main competitors. What differences are you looking for in applying for a job at this company?"

"We haven't called any of your references yet. Which one do you think would give us the most objective view of you as a potential employee? Why?"

"Your grades are a bit below those of the other prime candidates for this position. Tell me how you think we should interpret this difference."

Skilled interviewers are able to vary tone to explore various aspects of a candidate's responses and potential. Like an experienced actor, the interviewer weaves these various tones into an orderly flow of conversation that seems psychologically plausible. (The candidate, that is, shouldn't conclude that the interviewer is schizophrenic.) Unlike an actor's, the interviewer's chief goal in using a variety of tone is not to produce predetermined responses, but, instead, to elicit free, unguarded responses from the candidate.

VOLUME

How loud do you speak as an interviewer? You may not know. Research shows that speakers often misjudge their volume, usually erring on the "too loud" side. They mistakenly believe that they are booming out their words when, in fact, listeners can't hear all they are saying. Measure your own habits with regard to speaking volume against these three facts.

• *Most interviewers do not (but should!) adjust volume for the size of the room or the distance to the interviewee.*

Interviews in corporations occur in large board rooms, offices, and virtual closets, all with varying acoustics and seating arrangements. But the interviewer drones on, nonetheless, without a change in volume. We all know, from within, the sound and relative volume of our own voices—and make the false assumption that the same sound level is heard by any and all listeners in the room. Not so. Remind yourself to adjust volume for your environment.

• *In general, interviewees will not tell you that they can't hear you.*

The politics and etiquette of interviewing are such that interviewees will sit silently through almost any problem or annoyance rather than speak up. In Seattle, an interviewee for an insurance sales job sat for more than twenty minutes directly under a plinking leak in the roof without a word of complaint until the interviewer eventually noticed what she thought was excessive perspiration on the candidate. "I thought it was part of the interview evaluation," the interviewee sheepishly admitted later.

When interviewees don't hear your questions and comments, they go on anyway. Your impressions become falsely skewed by their apparent misdirection and off-track statements.

Learn to "hear" their silent protests by watching squinting eyes, knitted eyebrows, and a forward-tilted posture as signs that your volume should be raised. (A candidate's nervousness, by the way, can physically screen out incoming sounds. A bit of extra volume on your part can overcome this common barrier to communication.)

• *Too much volume is interpreted by interviewees as pushiness and hostility.*

Speaking too loudly can cause some interviewees to wilt. In feedback sessions after interviews they often blame the interviewer for "coming on too strong" and "getting uptight over nothing." Through their childhood years, these interviewees have associated a raised voice with reprimands and anger. That long association carries over to the interview room.

If you've been told by colleagues that you have a "strong voice," watch for otherwise unexplainable symptoms of reticence and timidity on the part of candidates. Back off the volume of your speech by degrees to see if the quality and quantity of their responses increase.

PACE

INTERVIEWEE:

"She wasn't really interested in what I had to say. The whole interview was just a ritual."

CAMPUS COUNSELOR:

"How do you know?"

INTERVIEWEE:

"You should have heard her. She talked so fast I could tell she didn't mean any of it."

This scene is played out weekly throughout the country. Interviewers from major companies have "their act down pat," and can blitz through the required questions in their sleep. The obligatory speech about the company and job opportunities is similarly committed to rote and delivered at a breakneck pace.

Why? Because interviewers lose interest in words they must repeat over and over, and have an understandable tendency to get through the task. In addition, interviewers forget that candidates have never heard the words before and will need time to understand them.

Pace, the rate at which words are said, influences how the candidate responds in the interview and how the candidate perceives the company. When the pace is too rapid, interviewees miss the question, ask for clarification, and draw unfounded conclusions about the company's "coldness" and "lack of interest." When the pace is too slow, candidates catch the contagion and slow down their responses. They conclude that the company is "stuffy," "dead," and "unprogressive."

For general interviewing purposes, interviewers should use a pace just slightly slower than usual conversation. (The slowed pace will emphasize the importance of the occasion and will help to compensate for the inevitable interference in attention caused by nerves.) To get a feel for this pace, interviewers can bracket off a passage of approximately 200 words. Read the passage in one minute to hear a moderately slow conversational pace. In actual sustained conversation we average about 225 words per minute.

Vary the pace of your speaking as a way of emphasizing important topics (in a slowed, deliberate pace) and de-emphasizing less important information (which can be dispatched at a faster pace.)

EMPHASIS

Particularly when we've been through the "script" of an interview many times before, we may tend to drone. The unrelieved sameness of our speech conveys lack of interest to the candidate and reflects poorly on the company itself.

Emphasis is usually marked by increased volume, higher pitch, and distinct pauses. Interviewers can put life back into their questions and comments by restoring appropriate emphasis to four areas.

Key Words

Interviewers working from notes can highlight key words in advance. In the following passage, imagine how much more persuasive the words are when emphasis is placed on the italicized words. (You may want to read the passage first without emphasis and then with emphasis on the key words marked.)

The company *understands* that there are many tensions that come with accepting a new job. You're saying goodbye to *close friends* and moving on to new *challenges*. In many cases, you're selling a *home* and looking for a new neighborhood, new shops, and *new friends*. That's why the company gives *special attention* to relocating new employees, making *sure* we do all we can to *help* you adjust to a new work environment and a *new home*.

Finding and emphasizing a key word in a candidate's response can provide a smooth bridge for clarifying or extending the topic at hand.

You mentioned ingenuity. What kinds of experiences in the past have given you the feeling that you were exercising your ingenuity?

Beginnings of New Topics

We all tend to remember what we hear at the beginning of conversations. What occurs later is often lost, as we tire of paying attention.

Use this natural inclination to your advantage by loading the "front end" of questions and explanations with important, emphasized words. In the following example, notice how the emphasized portion occurs early in the passage. The candidate will attend to the emphasized words even if he or she later loses attention as the explanation goes on and on.

You asked about flex time. In general, *the company works with you* to find a 40-hour per week schedule that fits your lifestyle. For most employees that means a schedule of four or five days during the week, usually 8 to 4 or 9 to 5. Some, however, choose to work over weekends. We have a night crew as well. *If you like extended vacation periods*, you have the option of putting in your 160 hours per month in three weeks, leaving you with a week off. *Up to four extra weeks* can be accummulated to be added to regular vacation time.

Summaries

In the middle of a long explanation the listener's eyes can begin to glaze over. Pull attention back to the topic by a summary sentence, emphasized by strong volume, heightened pitch, and appropriate pauses. Here are four examples of emphatic summary statements.

"Here's my point."
"So we're agreed so far to this point."
"Let me sum up before moving on."
"In a nutshell, here's what it adds up to."

Conclusions

Our last impression is often our most powerful memory. For that reason, interviewers practice placing special emphasis on their final words to interviewees. Consider the italicized words of emphasis in this close to an interview.

> We want you to know how much we *appreciate* your interest in this position and in the company. You've *shared* a great deal about your *excellent* background and abilities with us and we'll give that information *careful consideration* over the next few days. It's been a *pleasure* talking with you.

The candidate carries away a last positive impression of the company. Hired or not, he or she feels well-treated in the interview process and goes on to speak favorably of the company.

PAUSES

People great and small pause frequently in some of the most important communication experiences of life: accepting the Nobel prize, proposing marriage, or explaining the facts of life to the kids. Pauses serve at least three functions. First, they give our listeners time to consider our words (and hence signal that we think the words are worth considering). Second, they communicate our sincerity by giving the impression that we are carefully considering what to say. Finally, they set off one set of words from surrounding words for special attention by the listener.

To remind yourself how important pauses can be in interviewing, read the following passage first without pauses, then with pauses (perhaps two seconds or so in length). Notice how much more sincere and memorable the second reading sounds.

> Let me tell you a little about the company. (pause) TexRay Instruments was founded in 1972 on one brave idea (pause)—that the highest

quality instruments can always command the highest price. (pause) We began with electron microscopes. (pause) By 1980 we had moved into spectroscopy. (pause) Next year we're launching a new line that should push profits through the roof (pause)—magnetic resonance units.

In asking questions or giving feedback to candidates, interviewers can use pauses to create a feeling of spontaneity in what otherwise might be a dry, lifeless conversation. Notice the use of pauses in the following example:

INTERVIEWEE:

I studied COBOL, FORTRAN, BASIC, and C languages in my computer classes, but I've only had practical programming experience using BASIC.

INTERVIEWER:

BASIC. (pause) We still do some of our work in BASIC (pause)— instructional programs, that sort of thing. But most of our systems work is done in C. (pause) Remember much C?

ARTICULATION

Finally, words have to be said clearly and distinctly if they are to be understood and responded to. Steer clear of three traditional enemies to clearly articulated speech.

1. Words spoken quickly, often in excitement, tend to run together. For example: Wudjawannadayortotatriancallim? (Would you want a day or two to try to call him?)

This tendency is all the more pronounced in some interviewers with ethnic accents. Often we are the last to be able to hear our own verbal muddles—the words sound perfectly clear to us because we (unlike the interviewee) know what we're saying.

2. Words at the ends of sentences are often articulated poorly. We all think faster than we speak. Once an idea is partially expressed in words, our minds rush ahead to the next idea. The result, unfortunately, is a slurred, half-baked series of words at the ends of sentences.

To check your performance in this regard, tape record your next interview session. Listen to your strong, distinct sentence beginnings ("First, Ms. Phillips, I'd like to . . .") and compare them to your sentence closings (". . . anything else we can do.") If you hear your voice drop in volume and your articulation begin to slur you have "end-of-sentence slump." Jot down several of your sentences from the interview, then read them into the tape recorder with appropriate emphasis and articulation on the ends of your sentences. Notice the difference? Your interviewee will too.

3. The sounds b/p, m/n, t/d, f/s/th/sh are often articulated poorly.

We're all guilty of sliding over these consonantal sounds, particularly when talking quickly in casual conversation. Interviews, of course, share many of the qualities of casual conversation at times and therefore are full of these articulation potholes.

To brush up your articulation skills, read the following sentences several times with careful attention to the articulation of each sound. Don't let word sounds run together, especially if meaning is at stake (nitrate vs. night rate).

- Bob will be pleased to bill Paul for a better brand of pills.
- Tip big porters up at the pub beside the Pacific Boat Barn.
- Mention my name, Manny, and maybe no more mandates will come.
- One man may name no more than one nominee.
- Brad taught Dot how to do two double digit totals at one time.
- Tom's two dates don't demand total devotion to domestic details.
- A safe, soft thought is suited for those with something that seems thrilling.
- Thorsen Forest sends his spouse forth for the frosh/soph shot putt.

By careful articulation you give the interviewee a better chance to understand what you're saying about the company and to respond to your questions and comments.

PITCH

Like music, our voices rise and fall naturally in coordination with our meaning and level of excitement. In business situations, however, too many interviewers turn into "Johnny One-Note."

A tape recording of an interview session will clearly reveal any pitch problems you may have. Simply turn on the tape recorder in your office to catch a half hour or so of your normal conversation. Compare the pitch you hear there with the sound of your voice on an interviewing tape.

Some interviewers discover they are "Gravel Gertie," and need to speak "up and out," raising their chin a bit as a way of raising the pitch of their voice. Other interviewers hit a high note and hold it, producing, by the end of the interview, a sound effect not unlike fingernails on a blackboard. They need to drink some water, relax their vocal apparatus, and speak more calmly. These techniques are virtually guaranteed to lower the pitch of the voice into a more natural range.

PUTTING IMPROVEMENTS INTO PRACTICE

The work of upgrading verbal skills is much like remodeling a house. For the sake of those who live there, it's much better to take a room at a time. In the same way, target one or two aspects of the way you speak for improvement over the next few weeks. At first you'll feel self-conscious—"oops, I blew it again"—as you speak. But with patience and practice, those early failures will soon turn to more and more steady success. As you achieve your goals, set new targets. The dividends will surprise you: a new professionalism in the way you sound, a new respect evident in the way others relate to you, and much less frustration in correcting, repeating, and clarifying your messages.

CHAPTER 5

NONVERBAL TECHNIQUES FOR INTERVIEWING

In late 1987 a group of Santa Fe managers participated in an interesting experiment. In groups of three, they watched a five–minute videotape of a selection interview. The camera showed only the seated interviewer, both face and body. Importantly, the sound was turned off.

Based solely on what they saw, the teams were asked to reach consensus on an approximate "script" for what the interview was communicating to the interviewee. Here's a sample.

> She likes the interviewee at first and shows it in her smile and friendly conversation. But then something goes wrong. She must not like what she hears. She becomes more and more confused and frustrated by the interviewee and physically seems to retreat into a shell, with arms and legs tightly crossed. Her expression looks almost pained. At the end, with eyes pinched and lips tight, she tells the interviewee that he isn't qualified for the position and should look elsewhere.

Once the script was written, the videotape was replayed, this time with the sound turned up. To the surprise of all—especially the videotaped interviewer, who came in for the replaying—the scripts were almost all 100 percent offbase. The interviewer later told the managers that she had been quite pleased with the interviewee's performance and at the end of the tape was, in fact, encouraging his interest in the company.

How could experienced managers miss the mark so widely? They didn't. They, along with the interviewee, interpreted nonverbal signs accurately. It was the interviewer who missed the mark. She took a fool's bet—that people will believe our words even when our actions contradict them. In short, her nonverbal messages said "no" while her words were saying "yes."

I've demonstrated the dominance of nonverbal over verbal cues to audiences over the years by a simple experiment. I touch my forefinger to my thumb, forming an "O" and ask each member of the audience to do the same. Then I say, "I'd like you to place this O on your chin. " As I give these verbal instructions I place my own joined finger and thumb on my cheek, not my chin. Well over 80 percent of every audience will predictably follow my nonverbal lead rather than my verbal directions. The vast majority of Os go straight to the cheek.

Why do we believe what we see more than what we hear? Probably we have learned from childhood on that people exercise less conscious control over nonverbal signals that over their words. They give away their real motives and intent by a look in the eyes, a tension in their facial muscles, a twitch in their lips even when their words have been carefully rehearsed. The mere words "I don't know how the fender got dented!" didn't work for us as teenagers because our nonverbal cues were simultaneously screaming out our guilt.

THE HEART OF THE MATTER: CAN NONVERBAL BEHAVIOR BE CONTROLLED?

But can we grab hold of our nonverbal signals just as we have learned to control our words? For most of us, the answer is "yes, but." Yes, we can make great progress in managing our nonverbal skills. But feelings have a way of slipping out in spite of our best efforts—as Shakespeare said, "Truth will out." We will never, and perhaps should never, become such perfect puppetmasters of our own nonverbal behavior that not a look, frown, or twitch occurs without our willing it.

If complete control, then, is not a realistic option, we can

• sensitize ourselves to the language of the nonverbal messages we send and receive
• understand the confusion that results when we send mixed verbal and nonverbal messages
• orchestrate our message sending so that both verbal and nonverbal techniques cooperate in creating clear meaning.

EYE CONTACT

A candidate walks into the interview room. You glance up long enough to shake a hand perfunctorily, then look down to the resume and your list of questions. You look up again to notice how the candidate is dressed. You look down to a scoresheet mandated by the company. Preparing to ask a question, you look at your hands, then at the wall.

The eyes! That's where you'll find—and convey—more telling information than from any other source. We don't have to buy the romantic slush about "eyes as the windows to the soul" to insist that, in the first ten seconds of an encounter, the eyes begin to communicate five crucial bits of information.

- how nervous the candidate is
- how friendly the candidate is
- how confident the candidate is
- how bright the candidate is
- how alert the candidate is

Don't misunderstand. I'm not suggesting that you form ultimate opinions on these matters simply by looking into the candidate's eyes. How simple interviewing would be if that were so! But you do make initial judgments—first impressions—of these matters with those first important seconds of eye contact. And because we all like to prove ourselves right, we often use first impressions as hypotheses to be tried out and proven during the interview. In other words, we look for additional signs to bolster our early judgments.

Few of us are as adept at eye contact as we should be. The reasons are many. Some of us want to "manage by mystery" in the interview, withholding any eye-to-eye bond with the candidate as long as possible. Others think the interview is somehow more "objective," even scientific, if the interviewer's eyes focus on the wall, the window, or a particularly fascinating pencil on the desk. And for some, the stress of steady interviewing takes its toll—it's just plain hard to meet bushy-tailed enthusiastic job candidates one after another. There's an inevitable temptation to "hide out." The eyes escape from the interview even though the body can't.

In the face of all these understandable and quite human excuses, professional interviewers challenge themselves to establish and maintain eye contact because of the vast dividends.

1. Good eye contact helps us sort out hype from reality. We read feelings and compare them against the words we're hearing.

2. Good eye contact keeps both interviewer and interviewee in the "now," the moment at hand. Nothing is more discouraging in an interview than a rambling question or response, a grandfatherly stroll into the land of word salad. Eye contact keeps us from drifting.

3. Good eye contact encourages relaxation and sincerity. Especially when eye contact communicates interest and respect, both parties begin to shed their defensive poses and rhetorical bluster.

ACHIEVING GOOD EYE CONTACT

But how to do it consistently—there's the rub. Begin with yourself. Look into your own eyes in a mirror. The first thoughts have to be discarded—"getting older," "those little red veins," "what a nose." Get to the main event, what you see in your own eyes. (This experiment does require your participation. If you're not actually looking in a mirror, please do so.)

You may not be sure what you see. So act a bit. First, turn on a bit of anxiety. Notice how your eyes communicate your sense of foreboding? Now switch to relaxed, laid-back contentment—what a difference! Try keen, focussed interest. Notice how similar that look in the eyes is to a critical frown? How often have candidates misunderstood your eyes?

Getting to know and respect the communicative power of your own eyes gives you confidence to use them for assertive eye contact. You know what messages you're capable of sending. In effect, you know what candidates are seeing.

Once we turn away from the mirror to establish eye contact with a real person, of course, the game becomes much more complex. Now we not only serve up feelings through our eyes but have someone else returning the serve, often loaded with quite different feelings. We send out sincere, patient interest; we get back a look of discomfort and high anxiety. Now what?

This moment—when we receive the first reaction to our eye contact—is crucial for interviewers. The temptation is to respond in kind: you send me a look of anxiety, so I'll send you a quizzical, inquiring look to find out what's wrong. Then you'll send me a self-conscious look, knowing that I've noticed something wrong with you. And on it goes—the devolution of rapport.

Be sure enough of your own feelings, projected through your eyes, to hold on for a few moments. Don't flash mixed signals to a candidate trying to control nerves, make sense, and get to know you all at once. One interviewer whimsically refers to her "eyes of a St. Bernard—patient, caring, waiting for you to crawl out of the snow."

Natural eye contact that promotes sincere conversation differs from a stare in three ways.

• Stares look at another person; natural eye contact looks into another person.
• Stares hold on like a pit bull; natural eye contact breaks away occasionally to increase social comfort for both parties.
• Stares are fixed in one expression; natural eye contact allows a variety of feelings to develop and express themselves through the eyes.

AN EYE CONTACT EXPERIMENT

Convince your "significant other" that his or her cooperation in this experiment will be important to your career and influential in your gift-buying habits. Find a quiet spot where the two of you can simply look into one another's eyes for two or three minutes. (This isn't a game of stare-down; you may blink.) Watch for feelings as they develop and change. If you break down in laughter, try it again. After your three minutes of eye contact, talk about what you felt and what you perceived the other person felt. This is one quick, memorable way to learn much about the power of eye contact.

Other Uses of Eye Contact

In addition to encouraging rapport and sincerity, eye contact can serve three other common functions in interviewing.

Encouraging the Candidate to Extend or Clarify a Point
You don't have to say a word. Your direct look, combined with a moment of silence, signals the interviewee that more is expected.

Often this "silent inquiry" is preferable to a verbal request on your part. The former leaves the candidate free to shape further remarks in his or her own way, while in the latter you are intervening to define what kind of extra information you desire.

Revealing Approval of the Candidate

Explicit pats on the head ("That's quite impressive, Jack") have their place but can cloy if used too often in the interview. A sustained look of approval can be a nonverbal way of saying "that's great" or "I like your answer." Because nonverbal signals don't pin you down to specific judgments, you as an interviewer can feel more free to express negative opinions later without feeling that you have contradicted yourself.

Drawing the Candidate Back from
the Unproductive Rambles

Interviewees get to the point when you hold them in direct eye contact. When your own gaze moves to the ceiling or wall, their answers can become diffuse and rambling.

POSTURE AND BODY MOVEMENT

What attitudes and feelings do you associate with each of the postures in Figure 5–1? Twenty University of Southern California MBAs were asked the same question. Their most frequent answers appear upside down beneath each picture.

Chances are good that your judgments and mine are not far different from those of the MBAs. We've all been taught by the same teacher—everyday life. We know how the fat cats sit. We know how nervous jobseekers sit. We know how farm boys sit.

What we may *not* know, ironically, is how *we* sit, stand, and move during an interview. Our senses are directed outward, not inward—lacking mirrors or videotape cameras, we have little direct experience of what we really look like in action. (Hence the general distaste at being videotaped. For many business people, it is the first time they have ever really watched themselves from various angles in business circumstances.)

FIGURE 5–1
Postures Reveal Attitudes

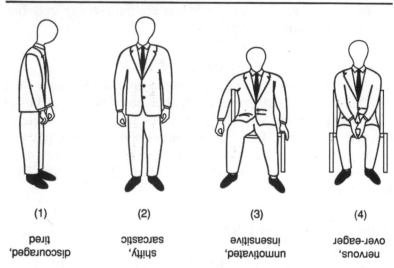

(1)	(2)	(3)	(4)
tired, discouraged	shifty, sarcastic	unmotivated, insensitive	nervous, over-eager

LEARNING TO SEE OURSELVES AS OTHERS SEE US

Burns said it for the ages: "Oh, that someone the gift would give us/To see ourselves as others see us!" Self-knowledge can be initially painful, but it provides the best handle we can grasp in changing ineffective habits.

If you have access to a videotape camera, simply tape two or three interview sessions with yourself in full view of the camera. Pay particular attention to your various sitting positions, the frequency with which you shift positions, your posture, your hand and arm movements, and your crossed or uncrossed legs. Take notes on signals you feel are being sent by your various movements during the interview.

Don't be misled, by the way, by popularized treatments of "what crossed legs mean" and "what your hands are revealing about you." No single movement absolutely means something about you, in the way that "stallion" means a "male horse." Body movements in interviews are much more like ballet, with suggested but not definitive meanings. The important thing is for you to locate the meanings you associate with certain postures and movements. What you conclude about your movements will give you insight into what conclusions you're drawing, consciously or subconsciously, about the movement of others.

Lacking a videotape, ask a friend to watch you during the course of a company meeting or interview. Ask him or her to jot down observational, not critical, notes about your posture and body movement. Review those notes with your friend, asking for any impressions he or she formed. As an example of this kind of exchange, here's a word-for-word transcript of an observation of a San Francisco food industry executive in a meeting.

> You looked fresh and professional at first, sitting comfortably and deeply in your chair. But as you became more heated in conversation, you kept repositioning yourself in the chair, as if you were really uncomfortable. Your movements were abrupt and jerky—leaning forward suddenly, then pushing yourself back. Toward the end of the interview you slumped back in your chair. I thought that you were either discouraged or that you had your mind made up. I noticed others in the meeting didn't direct their comments to you when you were sitting in that posture.

Hands are particularly revealing. See if you agree with the general attitude or feeling suggested for each hand position in Figure 5–2.

Many interviewers hide their hands during the interview session or busy them with note taking. In doing so, they fail to make use of one more powerful communication tool. If you are self-conscious about your hands while speaking, try the following "recipe" for effective gestures.

Step One
Keep your hands front and center, not under the table. If you wish, fold them on the table or touch them in the traditional "prayer" configuration.

Step Two
Just before asking a question, touch a button on your blouse or shirt with one hand—just as a way of getting it up and active. Then, as you ask your question, let your hand move naturally with your words. Don't worry if it falls back to the table before you've finished your question. You've used it to punctuate your words with visual support. You've added physical feeling and emphasis to verbal meaning.

FIGURE 5–2
Hand Language

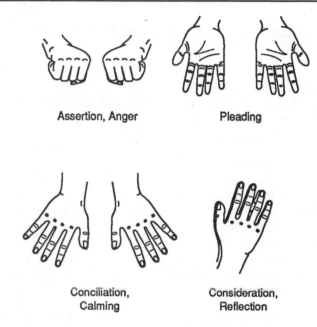

Assertion, Anger   Pleading

Conciliation,   Consideration,
Calming   Reflection

Step Three

Extend your range of gestures by "counting on your fingers"—that is, enumerating points by extending one finger at a time or touching them in order with the other hand. Use other visual interpretations of your meaning such as the "eraser," in which you briefly rub your fingers in the air as if erasing a previous comment or misunderstanding.

Step Four

When you're comfortable gesturing with a single hand, raise both hands into motion. A good starting gesture, particularly when asking a question, is the "watermelon" position. Simply hold your hands open and apart as if holding a watermelon. Talk to the interviewee through your opened hands, letting them drop at a natural point in your question.

Step Five

Now go for the big time with full arm gestures. Watch yourself and others in ordinary, spirited conversation for examples of these movements. Another good source for models are Sunday morning television preachers, though you may wish to turn down the volume, depending on your spiritual needs and personal tastes.

Interviewers who gesture freely and naturally get regular compliments from interviewees, colleagues, and superiors: "You keep things lively," "you really seem involved in what you're saying," "you make the company look good." These are big dividends from a small investment of energy and attention to movements that come naturally in everyday speaking.

FACIAL EXPRESSIONS

"I wasn't abusive or harsh in any way," the interviewer protested as, down the hall, a coworker tried to calm a weeping interviewee. "She just got more and more upset and finally broke into tears."

The interviewee had a different story: "I should have controlled myself. But he kept looking at me as if he was really disgusted by everything I was saying. You should have seen his face."

Second only to our eyes, facial expressions reveal more about our feelings and attitudes than any other nonverbal signals. In reviewing your own repertoire of facial displays, evaluate your use or misuse of the following:

Lips
Pressed, tight lips can communicate impatience, frustration, and nervous discomfort. Touching the tongue to the upper lip can signal suspicion and doubt. Pursing the lips (assuming a kiss isn't in order) can communicate shrewd, calculating evaluation. Biting the lower or upper lip (more of a trick) often signals tension over a transgression or faux pas on the part of the interviewee. The goal, of course, is not to repress lip movements but, instead, to make sure that the signals you are sending with your lips are indeed the messages you mean to communicate.

Chin
More than is usually recognized, the chin plays a prominent role in setting the tone for interpersonal communication. A jutting, defiant chin, raised imperiously, can communicate the interviewer's desire

to be viewed and treated as a superior. A buried chin can indicate grave reservation and suspicion. A "chewing jaw" sometimes signals general discontent with the interview conversation and a lack of involvement by the interviewer. Just as often it communicates to the interviewee that answers aren't being taken at face value but are being mulled over by the interviewer.

Cheeks

Puffing out one's cheeks, often with a burst of air, can communicate weariness, incredulity, or frustration. A tongue wandering about the inner contours of the cheek is similarly disconcerting to the interviewee. Without judging the etiquette of such on-the-job oral hygiene, it's fair to say that the tongue in the cheek makes the interviewer seem shrewd and calculating, often in a negative way.

Eyebrows and Forehead

This single muscular plate operates as one unit, with strong visual effect and potential for nonverbal meaning. Interviewers often lower their brows and knit their foreheads as a sign of intense concentration on what the interviewee is saying. Tip O'Neill's agonized expression of concentration provides a well-known example. The interviewer may even think that a compliment is being given to the interviewee—"look how much effort I'm putting into understanding what you have to say!" But compliments, like beauty, are in the eye of the beholder. What the interviewee sees is almost indistinguishable from a deep, disapproving frown. As an alternative to this ambiguous look of concentration, therefore, try to pinch the eyes slightly in concentration while smiling slightly. The combination will let the interviewee know you care about his or her responses without the confusion occasioned by the "concentration frown."

Interviewers develop an array of facial gymnastics that simply "feel good" in the course of a long series of interviews. The most obvious is the "eyebrow arch" in which the brows are raised as high as possible. What the unsuspecting interviewee sees is not a sleeping interviewer trying to stay awake, but, instead, a look of shock and surprise. Some interviewees have been known to quit an answer in midthought, wondering what caused the sudden look of shock on the interviewer's face.

Ears

Thankfully, the ears do nothing wrong in interviews. Why they are the constant prey of marauding fingers, then, is difficult to ascertain. In Italy, the "ear-pull" has a defined cultural meaning: "I'm on to you—don't try any tricks." But in the United States, ear pulling, ear cleaning, ear rubbing, and other forms of audio-erotic behavior are simply bad form.

DRESS

Both interviewers and interviewees are aware that one can under-dress and overdress for business interviews. We all try to find clothing that fits our tastes and personalities while also working advanta-geously for us within the particular business culture at hand. What we often underestimate is the effect clothing, appearance, and grooming can have in time-limited evaluation experiences such as interviews. William J. Young, personnel manager for Burson-Marsteller, a pub-lic relations firm, says appearance "is 65 to 70 percent of an inter-view." While it is certainly beyond the scope of this chapter to evaluate brooches and speculate on pinstripes, we can attend to the Five Commandments of Business Dress:

Thou Shalt Not Embarrass the Company

Are Levis appropriate in your business culture? Is a tie de rigueur? Are slacks advisable for women? The standard for judgment in such matters is not simply "what others are doing." You must determine what modes of dress best support the company's image, both present and future. Conversations with and observation of senior management can give you a good clue.

Thou Shalt Not Peacock Thyself

If you can afford a $2500 suit, fine. Have the good sense not to wear it to work. This stricture applies to jewelry as well. No matter what the dollar value, the item at hand should be judged by whether it adds or detracts from your performance and the interaction you have with others at work.

Thou Shalt Not Wilt

The rolled up, unbuttoned look may be comfortable toward the end of a business day. But this mode of undress sends all the wrong signals to interviewees: you aren't professional, you don't care much about their visit, you aren't making much money.

Thou Shalt Not Judge Interviewees Only by Their Threads

Granted, you can't help but be influenced by the smart, tailored look of a particular interviewee. Don't assume, however, that the less well-dressed candidate hasn't cared or tried hard enough. The economic realities of college and job changes leave many job candidates financially stressed. Make allowances.

Thou Shalt Plan Clothes in Advance

The business day is often a three-ring circus. The in-house buzz group that may require shirt-sleeves in the morning doesn't mean you won't have to don the mandatory blue suit, male or female, for lunch with an important client. Think through the demands of your day in selecting your wardrobe.

Interesting research by Robert A. Baron at Purdue University suggests that "efforts to enhance their 'image' can readily go too far." In his study, published in the *Journal of Applied Social Psychology* in 1987, an overabundance of nonverbal cues—including perfume, expensive clothing, jewelry, overt posture and facial gestures—actually reduced the candidate's ratings. Candidates can too easily dress for excess. "From a practical point of view," says Baron, "the best strategy for job applicants to follow appears to be one of careful moderation."

A PLEA ON BEHALF OF NATURALNESS

We began our discussion in this chapter by asserting that nonverbal signals are, by and large, unwitting and uncontrolled. Therein lies their power (for conveying feelings) and their curse (for revealing more than we wish). As we sensitize ourselves to what goes right and wrong with nonverbal signals, it's important to bear in mind the "centipede problem"—the dilemma of that curious insect which, turning its attention to each of its miraculous legs all at once, found itself unable to move.

Our model for working with our own nonverbal gestures should not be that of a puppetmaster pulling strings. Our performance in such a case will be jerky and unnatural. Better to have a "shepherding" relationship with our own impulses and nonverbal signals. We keep the flock together and moving forward as best we can.

Use the following checklist of nonverbal cues in Table 5–1 as an instrument for personal exploration. Based on your discoveries, set goals for bringing your nonverbal skills in line as powerful support for your verbal skills.

TABLE 5–1
Checklist of Nonverbal Skills

Use the following checklist to rate your own nonverbal strengths and weaknesses or those of a colleague. You may find it helpful to have someone who knows your professional work well fill out this checklist for you. Then you can compare your self-estimate with someone else's view.

	Poor	Fair	Good	Excellent
Eye contact?	1	2	3	4
Natural gestures?	1	2	3	4
Erect standing posture?	1	2	3	4
Comfortable, professional sitting posture?	1	2	3	4
Appropriate facial expressions?	1	2	3	4
Avoidance of unattractive nonverbal habits?	1	2	3	4
Attractive dress?	1	2	3	4

CHAPTER 6

ACTIVE LISTENING FOR INTERVIEWING

According to a Greek philosopher, "God gave us two ears and one mouth—and we should use them in that proportion."

Across industries and across types of interviews, the interviewer speaks only for about 25 percent of the session. The rest of the time he or she is hearing—and perhaps even listening. Executives spend between 45 and 63 percent of their day listening, according to William Ford Keefe's review of research in *Listen, Management!*

Ironically, most of us have never been trained to listen (even though we spent up to 90 percent of our time in formal education doing nothing but listening). We see the result around us each workday: those coworkers who look at us when we speak, but don't listen.

In earlier days of "theory X"—tough, authoritarian—management, the boss had no particular reason to listen. His or her task was to drive unwilling shirkers to put in an honest day's work. The boss had nothing to learn and much to impart. But, as Douglas McGregor makes clear in *The Human Side of Enterprise*, theory X management is quickly yielding to a new style, theory Y. Modern managers want inquisitive, mature employees who try to learn from one another. To set the pace, the manager tries to be that kind of person. In short, the modern "theory Y" manager has learned the value of listening to others.

And it's about time. The cost to American business directly attributable to poor listening is truly incalculable. The figure would have to include thousands of projects delayed, contracts rejected, clients misled, and plans scrapped, all owing to failures in listening at crucial moments. Probably the largest hidden cost to business of poor listening is employee turnover—employees who couldn't find a problem-solving ear.

Sperry Corporation, now Unisys, recognized the high cost of poor listening in its organization. Through a series of internal training programs and external advertisements, Sperry let the world know that its employees were ready and willing to listen.

That same inattention continues to plague the interview process. Good candidates slip through our fingers because we're deaf to what they're telling us. We hear but we don't listen.

This chapter can be considered a "listening bootcamp," pointing out the barriers and obstacles to listening as well as providing practical techniques you can use to improve your listening powers. The goal is to refine the fidelity of listening—in effect, to help you hear what you're missing.

For more suggestions on improving listening, see James J. Floyd, *Listening, A Practical Approach*. Glenview, IL: Scott, Foresman, 1985.

TYPES OF LISTENING

"I used to think of listening as a switch I flipped," recalls Roger Wyse, a manager for TRW. "I was either speaking or—flip—was listening. I missed a lot by that kind of either/or thinking."

Listening, like running, is a physical activity. We will ourselves to do it and put energy into the process. In the same way that there are distinct forms of running for different uses (jogging, sprinting, and so forth), so there are different forms of listening.

Free-for-all Listening

At the bargain basement level is purposeless, free-for-all listening. We have no particular goal in mind in this form of listening but simply let the incoming words wash over us as they will. Bits of flotsam and jetsam from the stream "stick," for whatever reason, and that's what we remember from the listening experience.

This kind of casual listening takes place in our homes, on airplanes, and (too often) in classrooms. It's listening in a mental hammock, rocking to the ebb and flow of the words.

Free-for-all listening has no place in interviews. For business efficiency and for legal reasons, interviewers must have clearly defined objectives in listening to and evaluating what candidates have to say. Anything less is to reduce interviewing to a slot machine: the candidate keeps cranking, hoping to stumble across a word or phrase that catches our attention and leads to a jackpot.

Listening for Facts

Though relatively simple, listening for facts is an important skill used widely in screening interviews, informational interviews, and technical exchanges. The goal here is to limit attention to certain facts—degrees, dates of employment, GPA, and so forth—and to hear them accurately. Interviewers practicing this form of listening consciously decide not to attend to the myriad of feelings and impressions accompanying those facts. In the immortal words of Joe Friday from "Dragnet," "Please, ma'am, just the facts."

In a "systems" approach to interviews in large organizations, it is often necessary, especially at screening and initial interview levels, to devote much of the interview to listening for facts. Companies like AT&T protect themselves from charges of bias by carefully training interviewers to attend to facts. Of course, later interviews assess attitudes, interpersonal abilities, and so forth. But the primary "cut" from among the job applicants is based on listening for facts.

Objective Listening for Attitudes and Feelings

A more complex form of listening involves "hearing between the lines" to perceive what the speaker feels. This form of listening is objective when we withhold an expression of our own feeling. In listening for attitudes and feelings, we do not usually ignore facts, but, instead, try to perceive them in the context of the speaker's attitudes.

For example, an interviewee's facial expression and tone while describing a previous job experience may reveal that the job was stressful. A skilled interviewer will pick up on such nonverbal and verbal clues as springboards to later questions.

Attitudes and feelings provide forecasts for the candidate's future performance and compatibility in the company. To make sure that interviewers assess such feelings, some companies define attitudinal categories on an interview evaluation sheet (See Box 6–1).

Box 6–1
Checksheet for Interviewee Attitudes and Feelings

In the space below, jot down your impressions of the candidate's attitudes and feelings, using the candidate's own words when possible.

The Interview

- How did the candidate feel about this interview?
- How did the candidate feel about people he or she has met in the company?
- How did the candidate feel about you, the interviewer?

Past Work Experience

- How did the candidate feel about previous jobs?
- How did the candidate feel about previous bosses?
- How did the candidate feel about previous subordinates?
- How did the candidate feel about previous tasks and assignments?

Present Opportunities

- How does the candidate feel about this job opportunity?
- How does the candidate feel about specific tasks and assignments included in this job?
- How does the candidate feel about the management order and style in this company?
- How does the candidate feel about his or her prospective compensation on this job? About benefits?

Future Planning

- How does the candidate feel about his or her career future?
- How does the candidate feel about the company's future?
- How does the candidate feel about increasing responsibilities in the future?

Empathetic Listening for Attitudes and Feelings

When the interviewer allows his or her own feelings to show in response to what the interviewee reveals, empathetic listening is taking place. The demonstration of feeling on the interviewer's part can be both verbal and nonverbal. If, for example, a candidate tears up at recalling a particularly traumatic life experience, the interviewer can "listen with" the speaker by words of understanding and appropriate facial expressions.

Empathetic listening implies a trust relationship between interviewer and interviewee and, therefore, acts to encourage ever-deeper levels of self-disclosure. In many cases, this amplification is desired by the interviewer and used in the decision-making process. But at other times, empathy opens a Pandora's box of highly personal information. More than one interviewer has stumbled into a morass of confession and personal revelation when showing empathy on topics such as divorce, child rearing, or health concerns. Except in the counseling interview, the interviewer probably does not want to play therapist for the interviewee. In these cases, the interviewer's expression of empathy must be kept in control as a way of controlling the candidate's flow of personal data.

Because of its power in interpersonal relations, empathy should be used discreetly and sincerely in interviews. Too much empathy distorts the interview process and makes objective evaluation impossible. Too little empathy encourages sterile responses and robot-like behavior on the part of the candidate.

Psychologist Carl Rogers has written widely and well on the power of empathetic, nonjudgmental listening. Truly listening to someone, Rogers points out, gives validity to that person. What the person says and what the person is are both treated as worthwhile.

BARRIERS TO EFFECTIVE LISTENING

"They're skilled interviewers," says a university career counselor of company representatives interviewing MBA students. "But I know they have trouble really listening after a dozen or more interviews in a row. I tell our students to sign up as early in the day as possible."

Most interviewers don't stubbornly decide to switch off their listening powers at a certain time. Three major forces conspire to lock the eyes and ears, the "doors of perception," in Blake's phrase.

Poor Listening Due to Prior Assumptions

The information and impressions that really get through to each of us have passed an elaborate set of internal filters. The most obvious case of such selectivity is in love relations. "Love is blind" in the sense that we choose to attend to aspects of the loved one that we find pleasing. If that relationship changes, a flood of additional, less pleasing data pours in, as is recorded in the annals of divorce court.

Examine your assumptions, therefore, about each interviewee who sits before you. Those assumptions may be severely limiting your ability to truly listen to him or her. Consider six myths that act as filters to what you hear.

The Age Myth
Some interviewers have unshakable expectations keyed to the candidate's age: "Interviewees under 25 are going to sound naive and idealistic, while those over 45 have little on their minds except retirement." Individual interviewers have noted the effects of age assumptions as they reviewed their hiring records over the course of several years. "I couldn't believe the figures," admits a Houston-based personnel executive. "My hiring clusters right around the 30 to 35 age bracket even though the ages of the hiring pool have been pretty evenly distributed. I think I tended to give the nod to people about my own age."

It may be instructive to detail just how the age myth influences our perceptions and eventual decision making. Mary Lou Morton, age 24, walks into our office. If we immediately identify her with a younger sister or "college kid," we establish a mental frame of reference—a scoresheet—against which she will be judged. One category, for example, might be "scatter-brained" (since our younger sister, also 24, gives new meaning to that word). We listen to Mary Lou Morton speak and decide whether or not she's scatter-brained.

Notice the devastating effect of the age filter: it has limited our "listening" to categories that Mary Lou didn't bring into the room with her, but that we, instead, imposed upon her based on our own assumptions.

"Listen to *me*, not to a typical 63-year-old grey-haired man," protested a systems engineer to a Silicon Valley interviewer. In 1982 he got the job and continues to be a mainstay in a successful computer chip operation.

The Culture Myth

Similarly, the interview process can be distorted by relying on inaccurate cultural notions. The computer industry in this country had to steer clear of a common, deleterious myth about Oriental applicants: "They're great at copying but can't come up with original ideas." Absurd—but a limiting factor in what we were able to hear Japanese, Chinese, Korean, and Vietnamese candidates telling us.

Culture, in the broad sense, can extend to socio-religious and regional backgrounds: "Mormons will give you 110 percent," "Episcopalians have a great white-collar network," "Jews have to have it their own way," and on and on. These destructive myths keep us from locating the right people for the right jobs.

The Sex Myth

Perhaps most pervasive of all, the sex myth continues to exclude capable men and women from jobs that "probably wouldn't work out" because of the interviewer's assumptions about sexual limitations. Those assumptions can be deep rooted. An industrial psychologist in Seattle related a typical case history: "This manager firmly believed that women, no matter how technically capable, would 'cave in' to harsh, hardball demands from clients. In actual fact, his mother was a kindly, can't-say-no woman. For over twenty years he based his 'men-only' hiring decisions for high-stress positions on her model. Only when the company faced—and lost—a sex discrimination suit did he work through his hang-ups in counseling."

Even when we admit a man or woman could do the job, we often base our eventual decision on the "fit-in factor"—how will Bill get along with the rest of the secretaries, how will Brenda take the rough language and horseplay on the loading docks? The status quo reigns.

Fair employment practices demand that we quit killing candidates with kindness, granting them unemployment rather than a sexually nontraditional job.

Poor Listening Due to Emotional Interference

An interviewer walks into the room carrying emotional baggage from home, work, and social life. Learning that the raise didn't come through, that the kid's braces will be $2400, that the clunk in the transmission isn't a minor adjustment all predispose the interviewer toward what Hemingway called a "black-ass mood." Candidates walking into that room are entering the lion's den.

Emotions of the opposite kind—affection, intrigue, and fascination—can be just as blinding. None of us completely outgrows the influence of a pretty or handsome face. But what Chrissy or Todd has to offer the company must be more than skin deep. Facing up to both negative and positive forms of emotional interference, the skilled interviewer sticks to the task of hiring by qualifications—legal ones.

Poor Listening Due to Competition

"A one-track mind" is standard equipment for human beings. If we think we can take notes, evaluate a previous answer, think ahead to our next question, and truly listen to the answer the candidate is giving at present, we're kidding ourselves.

Competition for our attention can take many forms: the clinking dishes in a smoky restaurant, the growl of machinery outside our office, the internal annoyance of cramps, the stifling weather, and so forth. To add to the challenge, many companies insist that the interviewers fill out one or more evaluation forms during the interview itself.

The candidate, too, is subject to competition from new faces, new surroundings, nervous sensations, and much more.

The answer is obvious: think through how, when, and where the interview will be given. Then, for the sake of good listening, limit those sights, sounds, and sensations that will compete with the candidate's communication. Completing the Interview Blueprint following Chapter 7 will help.

TECHNIQUES FOR ACTIVE LISTENING

Knowing the importance of good listening differs from knowing how to listen well. Here are eight techniques that work for interviewers who want to stay in touch and on track.

Nip Your Daydreams

Martin Luther complained that he couldn't recite the Lord's Prayer all the way through without his mind wandering to other images and topics. As the candidate speaks, be aware of your own mental vacations. Check in often to ask yourself, "Am I really listening?" Attention, like memory, can be trained to span longer and longer periods.

Make Connections

The perennial children's activity, "Connect the Dots," always reveals a picture of some kind as the payoff for accurate work. Play the same sort of game mentally with the ongoing interview. What is the candidate telling me right now? How does that connect with what he or she has already told me? What might come next? As in the children's game, a picture of the candidate will gradually emerge.

Mentally Talk Back to the Candidate

The interview game requires a reaction for every action. Instead of simply catching the words of the candidate, mentally bounce them back: conduct an internal argument with what the candidate is saying, think of examples or counter-examples, speculate on where the candidate is headed. You'll find that this active, though silent response will lead naturally to excellent "out loud" questions.

Pick Out Key Words

Not every word out of a candidate's mouth is golden—as you may have noticed. Actively search out the main words and phrases on which interviewee's beads of meaning are being strung. Listening for these "weighted words" can reveal much about a candidate's sense of order, logic, and coherence. The key words can also be useful for the interviewer in phrasing questions that apply directly to the candidate's background and interests.

Check Your Comprehension by Feedback

Are you catching what the candidate is pitching? Find out by occasional "playback" sentences. If, for example, the candidate has just finished a long response about career goals, you check your comprehension by playback: "You're saying that you want to move from technical functions into a managerial role as quickly as possible." The playback sentence need not be phrased as a question, though it may be. In either case, the candidate will probably let you know whether you've listened well: "That's right."

The technique of playback demonstrates your interest in the candidate in a concrete way. We all want to be understood, and we warm up to people who show that they've really heard us.

Be Comfortable with Silence

With friends, we are perfectly content to sit in silence for minutes at a time. No one feels an obligation to chat for chat's sake. If words come, fine. If not, that's fine, too. The friendship doesn't suffer.

We can impose the aura of friendship—our comfort with silence—on the interview process by not forcing ourselves or the candidate to fill every second with sound. John DiGaetani said it well in *Business Horizons*.

> One sure sign of a good listener is that he or she is not afraid of silence. Most people have a horrible fear of silence or are embarrassed by it, so they either chatter or encourage others to chatter to kill the awful sound of silence. But is it so awful? Paul Simon and Art Garfunkel heard a lot in it, and Mozart himself once said that the most profound music is silence.

THREE LISTENING EXERCISES

Nightly News

Use the active listening techniques discussed above as you watch a half-hour segment of the nightly news. Then answer the following questions to check your listening ability. (Checking your answers is easy: you either know the answer or you don't.)

    a. Describe how the evening anchor men and/or women were dressed.

    b. What was the second news story covered during the broadcast?

    c. How many commercials can you name or describe that took place during breaks?

    d. What can you remember about weather reports outside your region?

    e. Were there any "glitches" during the news? (wrong videotapes, camera on wrong newscaster, etc.)

    f. If a sports segment appeared on the news, which sports were covered?

    g. Did you detect accents in the speech of any of the announcers or reporters? What regions might these people come from?

    h. Geographically, what was the most distant spot mentioned on the news?

After you've played this game once, you'll notice an interesting aftereffect: the next time you watch the news you will "hear" the answers to these questions almost without trying. Apply this same phenomenon to your interviewing. Develop a set of interests that you key in on automatically as part of your general listening skills.

Your Significant Other

In your next conversation with your wife, husband, girlfriend, boyfriend (or whatever) resolve to listen more intently and completely than you usually do. Encourage disclosure by empathetic statements ("I certainly understand how you could feel that way") and frequent feedback statements ("So you felt angry when he said that"). After this experiment, discuss the matter of listening in your personal life. Ask your significant other if, in his or her opinion, you're a good listener. Go on to talk about what makes a good listener. Then apply those insights to your interviewing techniques.

What They Do Well

Complete the following chart by selecting coworkers and/or friends whom you consider good listeners. In Column B, jot down a word or phrase that names what they do best as listeners. In Column C, translate that skill into something that can be physically observed. An example follows.

A. Names	B. What They Do Best	C. Physical Manifestation
Phil Adams	patience	doesn't break in to change subject

Use the list of "symptoms" in Column C as your guide to behaviors that work.

A Potpourri of Poor Listeners

The Brain

This person listens only for the content of expression, never how it is said. As a consequence, he or she misses much meaning. If a colleague tries to explain why "there's a problem with George," the Brain leaps to a logical, but insensitive, solution: "Fire the jerk." Most questions are black and white for the Brain, who fails to listen for feelings and attitudes. Brains always have the answer, but only because they haven't understood the question or problem.

Jumpy

Like the Brain, Jumpy is impatient to express his or her point of view. Just watching the shifting, scratching, sighing, shuffling, stretching antics of Jumpy communicates the message loud and clear: "I don't care about you or what you're saying." Some Jumpy personalities may not really feel this way, but their nonverbal gestures belie their better intentions.

The Springboard

This listener waits for an attractive key word as someone speaks, then uses it to bounce to a new, unrelated topic. If the conversation is about auto insurance in Los Angeles, the springboarder will leap to a tiresome narration of his or her last L.A. business trip. The Springboard measures effective conversation by quantity, not quality: the more that's said on the most topics, the better.

The Pillow

This passive listener just sits there, motionless and inert. He or she isn't listening so much as vegetating. People quickly tire of speaking to the Pillow. The experience is rather like whispering a secret into the Grand Canyon—no response, no echo, no one home.

The Laser Beam

The direct opposite of the Pillow, the Laser Beam shows such ferocious interest in listening that he or she intimidates the speaker by long stares and pained expressions. Speakers fall silent under such hot lights because they feel judged, exposed, and threatened. Laser Beams know they can create a stage for themselves if they can first scare others out of the theater.

CHAPTER 7

THE RIGHT ENVIRONMENT FOR INTERVIEWING

Most interviewers—and most books on interviewing, for that matter—focus too narrowly on what's said, not where it's said. Interviewees, by contrast, are certainly as affected by the environment of their interviews as by the questions themselves.

With the permission of the personnel office, I placed a tape recorder in the waiting room during on-site interviews at a major Los Angeles accounting firm. Many of those in the waiting room were college friends. Here are some quotable quotes from what the just-interviewed had to say to the about-to-be-interviewed.

"The room is something else—paneled, oak furniture. Pretty impressive."

"They lead you down the hall into the holy of holies. It looks like the president's office or something."

"Get ready for the royal treatment—antiques, oriental carpets."

In an independent and certainly more thorough survey in 1987, 78 percent of interviewees exiting an interview mentioned aspects of the setting among their top three impressions. (Other frequently mentioned impressions were the demeanor of the interviewer—"He was very friendly"—and the candidate's own sensations of nervousness.)

THE IMPORTANCE OF THE PHYSICAL ENVIRONMENT

Especially in an era when Mr. or Ms. Right is hard to find and even harder to hold, "selling" the interviewee on the company is an important part of the interview. Every aspect of the physical environment affects that persuasion.

• *The waiting room:* Where does the candidate wait? What does he or she see on the walls and the coffee table? Does the furniture convey style, class, a "feel" of progressive, successful thinking and acting? (The interview environment can be unpredictable at times. Letitia Baldrige of *Complete Guide to Executive Manners* fame points out that the interview really begins when you first meet the candidate. She met and began to interview one of her best secretaries on the elevator. Impressions established there carried over into further meetings and a job offer.)

• *The walk to the interview location:* What does the candidate see as he or she walks through the halls by your side? Is your company putting its best foot forward? Or are you inadvertently taking the candidate past bored faces and slovenly offices?

• *The interview room:* Later in this chapter, we'll assess this important environment in detail, including chair placement. But for now notice its "first glance" characteristics. Consider a tottering stack of computer printouts, a bulging in-basket, and a bouquet of Post-it stickers on the telephone. What's the message? "No one is driving the bus at this place. Chaos reigns."

Physicians are more aware of this environmental influence than most business people. Notice that your personal physician places his or her credentials in full view. Everything about the office is calculated (or should be) to reassure you of the doctor's expertise. While businesses won't choose the same items to emphasize as a physician, they can make impressive use of

> civic and business-related certificates and awards
>
> original art or lithographs
>
> appropriate family or sports pictures
>
> well-photographed company products, services, or personnel

attractive sales charts, goal posters, and so forth

a window with an attractive view

Choosing the Right Room

Where will the interview be held? The answer for many managers comes with knee-jerk swiftness: "In my office, of course." That choice is traditional and still has much to recommend it: no scheduling problems, files and materials right at hand, and that general feeling of control that comes with one's own turf.

But at least consider alternatives before opting for this traditional location. In an exit interview with a disgruntled employee, for example, perhaps a neutral site—one that doesn't recall past arguments—will elicit information far different from that obtained "in the boss's office."

For Bob Nagel, central region sales manager for Owens-Illinois' Lily Division, the interview location really matters. "I don't want a person to feel as if he is outnumbered," says Nagel. "I don't do all my interviews in my office. Sometimes I'll meet candidates at O'Hare Airport. I rent one of the conference rooms there. This is a good technique because it puts the interviewee on an equal footing. He'll be more at ease and his answers will be more open and honest. In your own office, he sometimes feels like he's entering the throne room in supplication before the king."

Interviewing at a Meal

Or you can interview a candidate over breakfast, lunch, or dinner. The story is told of J. C. Penney that he first met job candidates at breakfast and always served them eggs. If a person salted or peppered his eggs before tasting them, Penney judged that the candidate was prone to making decisions without sufficient information—a "no-hire."

Without employing Penney's drastic test, companies can use the occasion of a meal to get more out of some interviews. First, meals are a relaxant for both interviewer and interviewee—the distractions of food and drink can break the clutch of anxiety for the interviewee as well as any undesirable aloofness or severity on the part of the interviewer. Second, the invitation to a meal says "special" to the candidate—royal treatment which can attract him or her to employment.

But the meal interview is not without its perils. Midlevel managers may be relatively inexperienced in how to eat and do business at the same time. In a 1985 survey by Accountemps, a New York placement service, midlevel managers average 50 percent fewer business lunches than upper management. In top positions, executives can average three or more business lunches per week. By contrast, only 10 percent of middle managers do business over lunch that often. Says Accountemps vice president Marc Silbert, high level executives "take the noon meal seriously. After all, they spend nearly eleven 35-hour workweeks a year eating business lunches."

In addition, more than one "over lunch" interview has been spoiled by the unpredictability of the site—crashing dishes, an irritating server, restaurant noise, or billows of smoke from an adjoining table. Lack of privacy can inhibit a candidate's answers as well as the interviewer's questions.

If you want the advantages of meal interviews without the disadvantages, therefore, follow a commonsense plan:

1. Select interviewers who know how to sandwich questions between sandwiches, so to speak.

2. Choose a quiet, private table in a restaurant with a predictably calm environment.

3. Conduct the interview in keeping with the social circumstance of the meal—little or no note taking, a conversational rather than inquisitorial style, and a de-emphasis on materials such as company charts and reports (which often can't be seen clearly in the dim light of a restaurant).

May Company eliminates the negatives of meal interviews by its frequent wine-and-cheese parties to heighten student interest in the company. Recently, at the University of Virginia, the company reserved Charlotteville's elegant Boar's Head Inn for an "international coffee" featuring fancy liqueurs and exotic coffees. Eighty prospective trainees heard the company pitch and met May Company executives in a relaxed, upscale, and impressive environment.

Interviewing at the Job Site

Particularly in light and heavy industry, job applicants increasingly are being interviewed around the lathe or assembly line. At Toyota's auto assembly plant in Kentucky, part of the job interview process is a simulated business experience. Teams of applicants are given a circuit board, a description of the company that makes the boards, and play money. They make business decisions which they later try to explain to company representatives.

Similarly, Robert B. Friedman, owner of Embassy Suites hotels, puts applicants in the position of on-site decision maker. "We bring the candidate in over a weekend and ask him or her to review the front desk. We ask what he or she would do to improve it."

Campus Interviews

Attracted by the numbers of students they can "process" in a short time, many companies visit college campuses regularly for dawn-to-dusk batteries of interviews. These have well-known but not insurmountable disadvantages.

• Interviews must be conducted in rooms made available by the college. These spaces often turn out to be little more than nondescript closets with a formica table and two institutional chairs. The image of the company can suffer.
• Interviewers weary from the steady flow of candidates, often scheduled every fifteen minutes throughout an eight-hour day. The interviewer's questions, responses and general interest level can become mechanical and insincere.
• The "impressers" present at the company's headquarters—luxurious offices, in-house dining facilities, and so forth—are usually missing from the on-campus interview experience. The interviewer, by his or her dress and demeanor, has the difficult task of establishing credibility with the candidate.

If your company participates in on-campus interviews, you can attack these problems successfully in three ways. First, work with college placement staffers to find the best rooms available on campus for interviews. By letting placement directors know how much you value the chance to give their students the best possible interviews, you can present your request for good rooms as a contribution to their program, not a critisicm.

Second, schedule interviews with frequent breaks for interviewers. They need this time to reflect, clear the head, and stay fresh.

Finally, spend the money to assemble a "dog and pony show" to accompany your interviewers. Just as you put together an eye-catching booth for trade shows, so you can design a portable display that interviewers can place in the interview room. This display in many ways takes the place of the attractive office environment the candidate would see at your company. Pictures of company projects, accomplishments, goals and policies can be included along with pockets for brochures. Your interviewers will be the first to appreciate this visual support to their efforts.

Unusual Interview Locations

Then there are the New Wave interviews—the "really-get-to-know-you" sessions one occasionally sees taking place on the racquetball court, the golf course, and elsewhere. Russell S. Reynolds, Jr., president of an executive search firm in New York, remembers an occasion on which

> I was interested in a young man for a key position in my company. Having learned from his resume that he enjoyed skiing, I invited him to spend a day on the slopes with me . . . I made it clear to him that the outing would give us a chance to size up each other.
>
> Near the end of the day we reached a high peak with an extremely difficult trail. Surveying the limits of our abilities, the candidate and I looked at each other. "What do you think?" I asked. He paused and looked down the trail again. Then, staring straight at me, he said, "If this is part of the job description, I'm not interested." He then descended the steep slope with apparent ease. His response said more to me about his judgment, sense of humor, and self-confidence than I could have extracted in a five-hour interview. He still works for my firm.

For managers who don't ski, Reynolds recommends that "the golf course, duck blind, tennis court, jogging trail, or even a quiet wooded path can offer similar opportunities for character insights."

In the discussion that follows, however, we'll assume that many, if not most, of your interviews take place at your company, probably in your office.

How to Arrange Seating

Gertrude Stein notwithstanding, a chair is not a chair is not a chair. Take a hard look, or even better, a hard sit, on what kind of chair you're offering to your candidate.

In many interviews, the manager stretches back on a $500 leather lounger while the candidate sits, all knees and elbows, on a hard side chair. His or her interview responses may reflect the seating arrangement—cramped, uncomfortable, and irritating.

Comfortable furniture, by contrast, helps the candidate relax, demonstrates the regard of the company and, most important, lets the candidate put his or her best foot forward.

One-to-One Interviewing

The single most important decision in one-to-one interviewing is whether or not to sit behind your desk. Certainly that position emphasizes an air of authority and "belonging" for you. In many interviews, this may be just the impression you wish to create (see Figure 7–1).

But, at other times, your desk may pose a real barrier to effective communication. Both you and the candidate can fall into unfortunate roles: you as the Judge and the candidate as the Accused before the

FIGURE 7–1

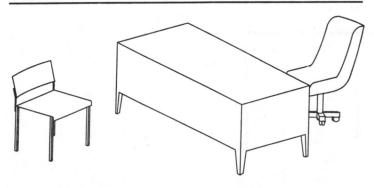

bar. The interview atmosphere can become inhibited, stereotypical, and dreary.

If you've always interviewed from behind your desk, take the advice of many skilled interviewers and at least experiment with a new seating position.

At Fletcher/Mayo/Associates, a Chicago advertising firm, Marji Gleeson says she "always sits on the same side of the desk as the interviewee since that's less confrontational." The seating pattern can take the form of two comfortable chairs placed at right angles. This seating arrangement is conducive to comfortable, low-stress conversation.

A bit more focused in interpersonal intensity is the pitched chair pattern. This pattern puts the interviewer and interviewee in close contact but not direct confrontation. Interpersonal feelings can be expected to become more intimate and personal as chairs are moved closer together and more distanced and "professional" as chairs are moved apart (see Figure 7–2).

The face-to-face pattern sets a no-nonsense, lay-it-on-the-line atmosphere for the interview. Neither interviewer nor interviewee has a desk or table to retreat behind. Signs of anxiety—rubbing of hands, crossing and uncrossing of legs—will be more noticeable than in other seating arrangements. Some candidates will be more prone to defensiveness; others, under the influence of anxiety, will tend to ramble on (see Figure 7–3).

What is the "right" seating arrangement for one-to-one interviewing? it depends upon the personalities and purposes involved. For the American Management Association, "there is no one proper relationship between your seat and the applicant's seat. Some interviewers

FIGURE 7–2

FIGURE 7–3

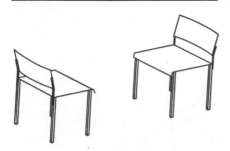

feel that desks create a barrier between them and the applicant. If this is how you feel, then the desk does indeed become a barrier. However, if you are comfortable seated behind your desk, then by all means sit there."

Group-to-One Interviewing

"I was interviewing for my first job," recalls Adela Oliver, a New York psychologist, "and when I walked in there were nine people sitting around the room. It was one of the most nerve-wracking experiences I've ever had. One of them would ask me how I felt about something, and I'd answer, and someone else in the group would disagree. They were trying to see if I'd change my answer."

Under the pressure of scheduling and money, group interviews are commonplace today. Estimates are far from exact, but two-on-one interviews in 1987 may account for as many as 40 percent of all first-contact job interviews. Executive recruiter Lynn Gilbert estimates that about 10 percent to 20 percent of her clients face interviews with groups of three or more.

Seating arrangements are crucial in group interviews. Where the participants sit determines whether the candidate will feel "me against them" or "one of the group."

In the panel form of group seating, the interviewers sit next to one another facing the candidate. In extremely formal interviews (including some military and disciplinary interviews), the chairs can advantageously be placed in a line to emphasize the high seriousness of the occasion (see Figure 7–4).

FIGURE 7–4

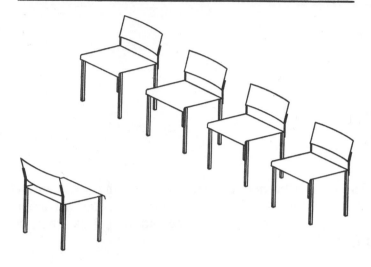

More often, the chairs are placed in a curved pattern in front of, but not surrounding, the candidate's chair. The curved pattern serves to soften the formality of the interview but still maintains the adversarial positions of interviewers versus interviewee (see Figure 7–5).

Because interviewers in a group panel usually know one another, they may tend to forget just how threatening a group-to-one interview can be, even to superior candidates. Putney Westerfield, chairman of Boyden Associates, tells of a time he sent a candidate to see a client about a $100,000-a-year job: "I didn't realize the executive who was the client believed in stress interviews. When the candidate arrived, they had three people start in on him. They told him, 'We received all this material on you and don't think you fit this job at all. What makes you think you could do it?' Of course the candidate was qualified. He didn't walk out on the interview, but he hated the company from then on."

In the circle pattern, the interviewee feels "one of the group." Interestingly, interviewers sitting next to the interviewee will tend to ask less threatening questions and even to defend the interviewee's point of view. Those seated across from the interviewee will be more confrontational in their questions and attitudes.

FIGURE 7–5

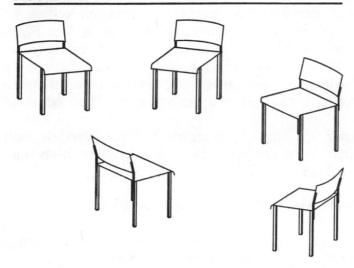

If your goal is to help interviewees "loosen up" for more forthright communication, the circle pattern will go far toward achieving that end. The flow of conversation will at times pass back and forth between interviewers rather than being aimed always at the interviewee (see Figure 7–6).

FIGURE 7–6

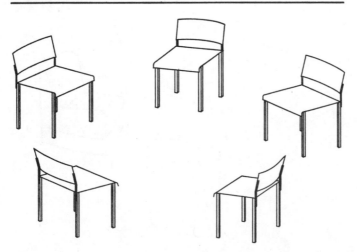

Most relaxing of all is the living room environment in which interviewers and interviewee find comfortable seating on couches and stuffed chairs arranged as if for friendly conversation (see Figure 7–7). Candidates can be expected to be most self-revealing in this environment. Viewed from another perspective, candidates in the living room environment sometimes reveal negative personal aspects that would not have emerged in a more guarded, "best behavior" environment.

In summary, the physical arrangement of the interview room affects both interviewer and interviewee. It determines in no small part the tone and emotional level of the interview.

Assessing the Human Environment for Interviews

But where to place chairs shouldn't overshadow a final concern in arranging the interview site: the human environment.

Consider the distraction of background noise, for example. Much of it—the clack of typewriters, the whirr of the elevator, the chatter of secretaries—may no longer be "heard" by interviewers used to

FIGURE 7–7

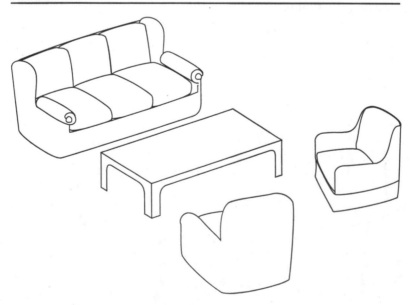

office sounds. But the interviewee may be thinking, "How do they hear themselves think in this place! It's hard to concentrate on their questions or my answers with all this racket going on."

Smoking, still a smoldering issue in many companies, should be resolved by firm policy: No smoking in interviews. Even candidates who become physically ill from tobacco smoke will hesitate to ask an interviewer to put out a cigarette. Nor is it enough for interviewers to ask at the outset, "Do you mind if I smoke?" Applicants will say "No, I don't mind," while inwardly bracing themselves for a physically uncomfortable experience.

Restroom breaks must be explicitly provided ("A drinking fountain and restroom are just down the hall, Jill. We'll break for a few minutes at 10 A.M.") This courtesy is especially crucial when a candidate has been scheduled for several interviews in a row at the company. Few job applicants will interrupt an interview for a restroom break; instead, they will squirm through questions, giving nonverbal signs that can be completely misinterpreted by interviewers as indications of insecurity, insincerity, or instability.

Finally, refreshments of some kind should be available in all but the most brief interviews. Coffee, soft drinks, or morning muffins bespeak the culture of a company. The president of North American Tool & Die, Thomas Melohn, says he determines "to make candidates as comfortable as possible, both physically and emotionally. I offer them coffee or a soft drink, and I never sit behind my desk. . . . The goal of all this is to encourage candidates to speak freely."

The message in a nutshell: Make plans beyond the verbal level— what questions you will ask—to arrange for the physical and human environments for interviewing. Stiff, awkward, and unproductive interviews can often be traced in large part to unattractive interview rooms, inhibiting seating arrangements, background noise, and too few provisions for human comfort.

The Interview Blueprint
Six Steps to Effective Interviewing

1. Interviewer Preparation

- Attitudes
- Verbal Techniques
- Nonverbal Techniques
- Active Listening

2. Needs Assessment

- What are the company's needs?
- What kind of employee fits those needs?
- What special tasks must be accomplished?
- What competencies are required to perform those tasks?
- What resources are available?
- How can likely applicants be attracted?

3. Environment Planning

The Physical Setting
- Reception
- Location
- Decor
- Seating

The Social Setting
- Number of Interviewers
- Number of Interviewees
- Refreshments?
- Formal/Informal?

The Time Setting
- Time of day
- Length of interview
- Timeline for decision

Comfort Considerations
- Parking
- Restrooms
- Breaks

4. Developing Questions

- Create questions (primarily "open") related to job description
- Create questions to assess applicant's intelligence, aptitude, motivation, skills, personality, experience, and goals
- Arrange questions in a balanced, meaningful sequence
- Review all questions for legibility
- Develop instruments for recording and evaluating applicant responses

5. Conducting the Interview

The Warmup

- Put the applicant at ease by small talk and by the use of low-threat, high-interest questions

The Contract

- Specify what the interview is for, what topics will be covered, and how information will be handled

The Interview Body

- Pose questions, listen actively, probe for facts and feelings

The Conclusion

- Sum up, solicit questions from the applicant, express appreciation, tell what will be the next step

6. Following Up

- Complete all interview records
- Compare applicant records
- Consult with stakeholders
- Decide upon a candidate
- Justify selection in writing

CHAPTER 8

THE STAGES OF
EFFECTIVE INTERVIEWS

"Develop interview questions? Not on your life," says John T., a midlevel manager with a large architectural firm in the Northwest. "I never know what I'm going to ask a job candidate until I meet him or her. All the spontaneity and sincerity goes out of interviews when questions are planned and written out in advance. I like to wing it."

Perhaps John is one of those rare interviewers who ask just the right question at the right time, as if by nature. The rest of us aren't so fortunate. Good interview questions don't simply pop into our minds. This chapter, then, is for the vast majority of interviewers who, before the actual interview, want to understand

- What they will ask.
- Why those questions are important.
- How they can record and use the results for decision making.

WHAT IS A GOOD INTERVIEW QUESTION?

Interview questions can vary from long technical explorations to a one word query, such as "Why?" or "When?" or "How?" But all good interview questions share five crucial attributes.

Each Question Should Have a Purpose

The interviewer designs questions to achieve certain ends—most often to elicit data for decision making. Whether broad or narrow in scope, each question should be aimed at a target of some kind.

Yes: Are there any circumstances that will prevent frequent out-of-state travel for you? (This question is aimed at a specific target; determining availability for travel.)

No: Do you have children to care for? (This question—an illegal one—has no clear, business-related purpose.)

Each Question Should Be Tied to Job Requirements

For both legal reasons and simple efficiency, interview questions should not stray into areas unrelated to the job. Interviewers can, of course, ask "getting-to-know-you" questions—but even these should try to draw out personal characteristics and attitudes important to success in the company.

Yes: How would you feel working for one of the smaller companies in our marketplace? (This attitudinal question tries to elicit the candidate's entrepreneurial instincts.)

No: Most of us have season tickets for the Rams. You're a football fan, aren't you?

Each Question Should Be Focussed and Clear

Perhaps as much as 25 percent of interview time across industries is wasted on wandering, inprecise questions from interviewers. Poor questions, in turn, produce confused, misdirected answers from interviewees. The company, the interviewer, and the interviewee all stumble.

Yes: What aspect of selling do you enjoy most?

No: Selling means different things to different people. We all have different feelings about it, I guess. What I'd like to know is if, or whether, you've given any thought to pros or cons, particularly the pros, associated with it.

Each Question Must Be Repeatable

If winners and losers are to be determined fairly, interviewers must see that all interviewees have approximately the same chance to strut their stuff. Interview questions, therefore, must be general enough to apply to all candidates.

Yes: What influenced you to consider a career in human resource management?

No: Both your parents were professional labor negotiators. How did they influence your career goals?

Each Question Should Have a Meaningful Place in the Entire Sequence of Interview Questions

Poor interviews hopscotch all over the map, from personal to professional questions, from narrow to broad concerns, from skills to attitudes. What gets lost in the process are the necessary bonds of sincerity and trust between interviewer and interviewee.

"We had the embarrassing experience," says a personnel director for a San Francisco telecommunications firm, "of finding Mr. Right—only to have him reject our offer. His interviews, he told us, gave him a less than favorable impression of the company. He decided to look elsewhere."

In successful interviews, questions follow a meaningful sequence. Thoughts join to thoughts in both logically and psychologically acceptable ways. A question about the candidate's college experience, for example, links to a question about carryover skills from college to the workplace. By such links, the interviewer indicates "I understood you and am interested in you" to the interviewee.

HOW TO DEVELOP GOOD INTERVIEW QUESTIONS

While books on interviewing—including this one—often contain many sample questions, the most useful interview questions grow out of a development process such as the following eight-stage plan.

STAGE ONE. MAKE A LIST OF COMPETENCIES BASED ON THE JOB DESCRIPTION

Competencies include knowledge, skills, personal traits, and abilities necessary to perform the job successfully. In short, what must the successful candidate be able to do? In listing these competencies, look closely at working conditions, major duties, expected job outcomes, and your company culture.

Sample competencies for hiring a newsletter editor include

1. Ability to write and to edit at a professional level in journalistic format
2. Ability to manage a team of writers, photographers, and production staff
3. Ability to gather ideas, goals, and information from other department heads

Note that these competencies will form the groundwork for interview questions. You'll know what to ask because you know what you're looking for.

"People weed out and toss away resumes of some of their best potential candidates," says Andrew Sherwood, CEO and president of Goodrich & Sherwood, a human resources consulting firm based in New York. Interviewers, he says, make the mistake of settling too early on criteria—"We want a person with a finance major in college"—and then rush through resumes eliminating those that don't match up exactly. Instead of beginning with absolute criteria, he suggests, decide what responsibilities you need filled.

For Millie McCoy, managing director of Gould & McCoy, Inc., this task involves asking

* What are the responsibilities involved?
* What abilities does someone need to carry out those responsibilities?
* How much experience is needed?
* What kind of culture does the organization have?

The Ideal Applicant

Industry Week recently drew up two lists—those traits that, across industries, are considered indicative of an ideal employee and a companion list of undesirable traits. You may disagree with these listings—but so much the better if they stimulate you to form your own list for your own hiring needs.

Ideal Profile
Achievement-oriented, success-oriented, recognition-oriented, goal-oriented, teamwork-oriented, pride, accomplishment-oriented, will-

ing to compromise, less critical/vindictive, less need for sympathy, fewer emotional needs, requires less attention, less restless, perseverance, resolute, creative, independent, religious background, flexible, involved, obliging, accommodating, open-minded, empathetic, good family background, strong work ethic, a leader.

Negative Profile

Desire to be led, aggressive, critical/vindictive, restless, uncertain, uninterested, low productivity, happy-go-lucky, rebellious, antiestablishment, injury-prone, cause-oriented, poor work history, under 18 without work history, bullheaded, needs emotional support, no tenacity, poor family background, poor community environment, single, single parents, financial problems, vocal, divorced, staunch, stubborn, hardheaded.

STAGE TWO. ESTABLISH OBJECTIVES FOR THE INTERVIEW

What do you want the interview to accomplish? In the case of the newsletter editor above, we may want to achieve at least four objectives.

1. To determine the candidate's ability to perform competencies (potential).
2. To determine the candidate's willingness to perform job competencies (motivation).
3. To provide information about the job and the company.
4. To assess the individual's "fit," including communication skills, with current company culture and personalities (compatibility).

Jeff Latterell, senior personnel development specialist at Dravo Corporation, offers a helpful "hunting ground" of areas for inquiry in an interview. From among these, select those areas that are "musts" (i.e., objectives) for your interview situation.

1. Responsibilities and duties of the job.
2. Salary and benefits.
3. Working conditions.
4. Supervisor's style.

5. Candidate's personality.
6. Candidate's attitudes.
7. Candidate's ability.
8. Candidate's potential.
9. Candidate's success in previous positions.
10. Candidate's ability to fit in with others in the department.
11. Candidate's ability to perform specific jobs.
12. Candidate's interests.
13. Candidate's dependability.
14. Future opportunities for candidate within the organization.
15. Stability and security of the position.
16. Salary desired by the candidate.
17. Qualities desired in an employee.

Senior personnel officers at an Ohio insurance company relate a major change in their interviewing procedures. "We used to spend 5 percent of our time figuring out what kind of employee we wanted to hire and 95 percent of the time interviewing applicants. Now we spend 25 percent of our time making sure we have a clear picture of whom we want to hire. Our interviews, as a result, are much more focussed and successful."

STAGE THREE. DESIGN INTERVIEW QUESTIONS FOR MAJOR JOB COMPETENCIES.

You know what your ideal employee will have to do (competencies). You know as well what the objectives of the interview are. Now you must create specific questions that will sort out the sheep from the goats.

To achieve your objectives, these questions will test not only "can do" skills (potential) but also "will do" abilities and attitudes (motivation) as well as compatibility.

Writing in *Working Woman*, Robert Half suggests that questions be divided into four areas of inquiry: experience and skills, general intelligence and aptitude, attitudes and personality, and education. (Questions in the interview, of course, are not necessarily asked in this order.) Here are questions he has found particularly successful in each of these four areas.

Experience and Skills

- What is your boss's title, and what are your boss's functions?
- Can you describe for me a typical day in your job?
- Tell me about the people you hired in your last job. How long did they stay with you, and how did they work out?
- What do you consider the single most important idea you contributed or your single most noteworthy accomplishment in your present job?
- How would you install a standard cost-accounting system?
- What do you think it takes for a person to be successful in (fill in the specialty)?
- If you run into this situation (give a typical problem situation the candidate might be expected to deal with as an employee) how would you handle it?
- What specific strengths did you bring to your last job that made you effective?
- What specific strengths do you think you can bring to this position?

General Intelligence and Aptitude

- Can you tell me a little bit about how you make important decisions?
- What are some of the things your company might have done to be more successful?
- What do you know about our company?

Attitudes and Personality

- Could you tell me why you're interested in this job?
- Why have you decided to leave your present position?
- What would you like to be earning two years from now?
- What have been the biggest failures or frustrations in your business life?
- What risks did you take in your last few jobs, and what was the result of those risks?

- Think about something you consider a failure in your life, and tell me why you think it occurred.
- How did you enjoy working for your former employer?
- What do you do when you're having trouble solving a problem?
- What did you do in your last job to make yourself more effective?
- Where do you see yourself three years down the road?
- Tell me about your hobbies and interests.
- Describe the best boss you ever had.
- What kind of references do you think your previous employers will give you?

Education

- Why did you decide to go (or not to go) to college?
- Tell me a little about how well you did in school.
- What were your best and worst subjects?
- What sort of jobs did you have while you were at school?

Open Questions

Note that none of the foregoing questions can be answered by a simple "yes" or "no." The candidate has to reflect, formulate, and express— the very skills you want to see demonstrated. Such questions are called "open questions." By contrast, a question like "Have you ever managed others?" is a closed question, requiring only a yes/no response. Open questions guarantee that the interviewee, not the interviewer, will do most of the talking during the session.

One especially important group of open questions is clarifying questions. Interviewers often assume, incorrectly, that they immediately understand what the candidate is trying to tell them. Through clarifying questions, the interviewer gives up that assumption. He or she consciously entertains the possibility that the candidate has been unsuccessfully or incompletely understood. The interviewer uses clarifying questions ("Please explain more fully why," "Specifically how did you," "What did you mean in your earlier comment that") to check understanding and deepen inquiries.

Sample Open Questions

"How did you handle discipline problems?"
"Why do you want to make a job change?"
"What specific aspects of your last job challenged you the most?"

Different Questions for Beginners and Experienced Applicants

In some hiring situations, you may want to develop alternative questions based on the applicant's degree of experience. *Supervisory Management* recommends the following type of questions for applicants just out of college:

What are your special abilities?

What were some of your extracurricular activities in school?

What have you learned from your summer jobs?

What have you done that shows initiative (or the ability to get along with others, meet the unexpected, or be persuasive)?

What would you expect to do on your first day?

For more experienced applicants, the following open questions are more appropriate:

What evidence can you give of your success in selling (research, establishing a new department, administering budgets, or whatever)?

What difficulties did you have to overcome when you took over as production manager? How did you do it?

Listening for Success and Fulfillment Needs through Open Questions

An applicant's responses to open questioning will tell you much about the person's needs, says Linda Richardson, founder of the Richardson Group, a Philadelphia training firm. The applicant will reveal his or her success needs in using terms of money, power, and status. Richardson asks questions like "What things are important to you in your career development?" to get at this level of need.

But more important, she says, are fulfillment needs—what the applicant needs in terms of personal satisfaction, peer relations, reporting structures, emotional climate, and loyalty to and from the company. If the applicant doesn't volunteer insights into these areas, Richardson asks, "What else is important to you in your situation?"

"If you don't cover these two major areas," she warns, "you're going to miss who the person is."

Using More than Your Voice for Questions

Some open questions involve a prop or short document. Pechner, Dorfman, a firm specializing in personnel selection, hands an idealistic, four-paragraph employee policy statement to applicants. The interviewer then observes or asks for their reaction. The results can be telling.

About 10 or 15 percent, according to Stephen Cabot, a senior partner with the firm, lay down the statement without reading it or asking about it. Cabot takes this action as a sign of apathy. About 25 percent will read the document, chuckle, then hand it back. This, for Cabot, is also a negative because it indicates an inability to express real feelings.

Another 20 percent, he says, will read the document, then over-react, saying something like, "This is the greatest company in the world. I've dreamed of working for a company like this." Cabot says that this kind of applicant definitely should not be hired. The response lacks sincerity and judgment. The final 20 percent will respond more honestly: "I don't have any trouble with that; it sounds good." This measured, truthful response is considered a positive sign.

Closed Questions

"Yes/no questions" are not forbidden in interviews, but they must be limited in number. Otherwise, the interviewer will be doing all the formulating, expressing, and information sharing—the very skills you want the candidate to demonstrate.

Closed questions are used most often for checklist concerns: "Have you filled out the EEOC form?" "Did Dr. Evans assign a time for your health exam?" Whenever possible, keep these housekeeping questions outside of the interview itself. Often they can be handled by a secretary or a phone call.

Avoid closed questions that seem to include their own answer. Michael Ahearn, manager of central staffing for Apple Computer, gives these examples of such "answer-prepaid" questions: "Would you say that you have good interpersonal skills? Was getting your MBA from Stanford a positive experience for you?" Of course, applicants will answer "yes."

By contrast, a valuable kind of closed question is the verification question. In this form of questioning, the interviewer repeats in his or her own words what they think the applicant has said. Here are typical verification phrases: "If I understand you correctly, you're saying," "What I hear you saying is that," "Are you suggesting that." Strictly speaking, these verification statements are "closed" in the sense that the applicant can answer them with a simple "yes" or "no". But because verification questions demonstrate interest in what the candidate has said, they often produce quite "open" answers— additional explanations or examples from the applicant.

Sample Closed Questions

"Have you definitely decided to take the CPA exam?"

"Are you physically able to move 80 pound cartons?"

"Will you consider a salary offer between $30,000 and $35,000?"

Beware of False Inferences Drawn from Facts

Perhaps the most common problem in using closed questions is not the answer received from the applicant, but, instead, the inaccurate inferences drawn by the interviewer. Vincent Loretto, a school superintendent writing recently in *Personnel Journal*, points to costly mistakes his interviewers sometimes make by false inference.

> Too often questions are asked; honest answers given; and invalid inferences drawn. . . . Here are examples of invalid inference drawn during interviews.

- Fact: Knows subject matter. Inference: Can teach subject.
- Fact: Attended small, private school and is from rural community. Inference: Can't teach in an urban setting.
- Fact: Of same cultural and socio-economic background as pupils. Inference: Will command respect of pupils.
- Fact: Big, strong, star athlete. Inference: Can handle 'tough kids'.

When using closed questions to gather facts, be careful not to extend inferences into areas that can only be explored by open questions.

Developing Questions from a Resume or Application Form

Well before the interview, you will no doubt have reviewed the applicant resume or application form with care. These documents can provide the basis for some of your best—and most telling—interview questions.

But beware. Jeff Davidson, vice president of IMR Corporation of Washington, D.C., cites a leading U.S. employment agency's opinion that "nearly 80 percent of all resumes contain some misleading information, usually in the area of employment history. The most common misrepresentation occurs when candidates fabricate names of firms they worked for to cover long gaps of unemployment."

Here are probes that can help you sort out fact from fiction in the interview.

Employment

Candidates frequently give job histories by years rather than by month and year. In such cases, a three-week summer job can be inflated into what seems a full-year position. For key experiences, ask the applicant exactly how long he or she worked for the company. Was employment full-time or part-time?

Job titles, too, can be inflated far beyond the actual responsibilities they entailed. When a job title on the resume sounds suspiciously grandiose, ask the candidate if the job title on the resume was in fact what the position was called in the company. In telephone follow-ups with employment references, check for confirmation. This simple step is an effective measure of the applicant's integrity. A "white lie" on a resume often portends a future course of dishonesty in your employment, ranging from fudged expense accounts all the way to embezzlement.

Education

Many applicants now play fast and loose with their "major" and "minor" in college. Be especially cautious of terms like "emphasis in finance" or "economic sequence" after the listing of BA or BS. Did the applicant really major in finance? If not, what does "emphasis" mean? Two or three courses? Confirm the candidate's representation of this matter by reference to his or her transcripts or by a call to his or her college.

Grade point averages can be stated deceptively, if not dishonestly. A student may use an overall GPA, including general education courses, to represent academic success in the major. A student who got As in general courses can thus hide a series of Cs during the crucial junior and senior years. If you are concerned about academic preparation, ask the applicant to name five or six courses taken as part of the major, with grades for each.

Applicants can also create false impressions of when they will finish their college degree. Ascertain 1) how many courses they must yet complete, and 2) if and when they are registered to take those courses. Loose phrases such as "now completing my senior year" and "within a few months of completing my degree" often disguise the actuality: a part-time student who may be a year or more away from graduation.

Good application forms can go far toward pinning down applicants to the real facts of their preparation. A sample application form can be found on pp. 153-157.

STAGE FOUR. DEVELOP A WAY TO RECORD IMPORTANT ASPECTS OF APPLICANTS' RESPONSES

As applicants respond to your questions, you need some way to keep score. If you plan your scorekeeping materials with care, you will have an excellent way to compare candidates in detail.

Begin by listing things to look for in candidates' responses for each question. If, for example, you plan to ask an applicant "How can you motivate employees?", you might create a brief scoresheet as follows:

Candidate supports answer by referring to. . .
Money
Peer pressure
Favoritism
Perks
Personal attention/warmth
Team spirit
Fear
Other

Where does such a scoresheet come from? Directly from your best guess as to what applicants would say—including what the ideal applicant would say. In the example above, you may decide in advance that your ideal candidate will emphasize motivators other than money.

You may also want to keep track of how the candidate supports his or her points. Are all answers theoretical ("What I would do, what I think should be done") or can the candidate point to practical examples ("What I did")?

Here is the way John T. Hopkins, manager of sales at Dunhill of Rochester, Inc., structures his scoresheet. Hopkins provides a guide to responses for each major question he asks in the interview. Notice how much guidance this lively evaluation form could give to another, perhaps less experienced interviewer in the company.

Question 1: What brings you to this agency?

- I saw your ad in the paper. [Excellent.]
- Sue McIntyre, a friend, recommended you. [Also excellent.]
- I saw your listing in the Yellow Pages. [Registered every-where, eh?]
- You have a great reputation. [Stop the malarky!]
- My company's personnel manager recommended you. [Fired? Could be OK.]

- I was in the building and saw your sign. [Again excellent: an honest person.]

Comment: Learn to cherish honesty, rather than answers designed to please you.

Question 2: What sort of a job are you looking for?

- Oh, I don't know. What's available? [Ugh!]
- I'm interested in management. [Likewise ugh.]
- I saw your ad for a space buyer. [Excellent.]
- The Dewappo Company needs an accountant. I'm qualified. [A bonus!]
- I'm tired of my present job. [Tired—or fired?]
- We're getting married (or having a baby or buying a house), and we need more money. [Good motivation.]

It goes without saying that your record-keeping materials should not be shown to the candidate. Nor should they be used in an obtrusive way, attracting eye contact that should be given to the applicant.

The Weighted Evaluation Form

Especially when interviewing many applicants, a weighted evaluation form can make comparison of candidates more accurate and objective. Note that the portions of the form in parentheses are filled in during or after the interview, while other parts are completed in preparation for the interview.

The Importance of Record Keeping

Why keep such records? First, new legal guidelines from federal, state, and local authorities constrain employers to base hiring, performance appraisal, discipline, and termination procedures on objective, recordable data rather than on impressions. Modern personnel offices often spend more time demonstrating to such authorities why they didn't hire someone than why they did. When such explanations are necessary, the scoresheets filled out by interviewers can show that each candidate was evaluated by the same standards.

Beyond legal reasons, record-keeping materials help interviewers make better decisions among competing applicants. Especially

Name of applicant:
Date:
Interviewer(s):

Job Requirement	Applicant's Demonstrated Abilities	Importance Factor		Score	Total
Resolve conflict among employees	(Former labor negotiator, 5 years)	3	×	(4)	(12)
Writing ability	(B.A., English)	5		(4)	(20)
Team-building ability	(Good references for team leadership)	5		(5)	(25)
Budget management	(Managed $1.5 million budget, 3 years)	4		(4)	(16)
		TOTAL		73	

when interviewing more than three or four applicants, the amount of interview data to be retained in the interviewer's head becomes dizzying. Too often final selection is based on "gut feeling"—"Mary Jo just seemed right for the job"—rather than a careful review of competencies.

When more than one interviewer sees the same applicant, a common record-keeping scheme can prove invaluable for comparing impressions and coming to consensus.

Can you afford the time to develop a scoresheet for interview questions? As suggested in Chapter One, you can hardly afford not to. Interviews based on intuition have a notoriously poor track record for selecting successful employees. The time invested in thinking through what you're looking for and how you'll know when you find it is repaid many times over by better hires.

STAGE FIVE. ARRANGE QUESTIONS IN A BALANCED SEQUENCE

At this point you know what you want to ask, why you want to ask it, and how you'll record the results. Now visualize the actual interview.

How many questions should be asked in a particular topic area? In what order should questions be asked?

There are, of course, many possible scenarios for interviews. The two most common are structured and nondirective.

Structured Interviews

As described in the stages above, questions in a structured interview are determined and arranged in advance. This type of interview is used most often for initial interviews and for clerical-level hiring.

While structured interviews have the marked advantage of an organized plan—what to ask, when to ask it, and what to do with the results—they can seem too formal and restrictive for some business situations.

Nondirective Interviews

At such times, the nondirective interview may be more appropriate. In this type of interview, the interviewer has general areas of interest but no preformed, sequenced questions for the interviewee.

In the ideal nondirective interview, the interviewer hopes to discover not only expected data (the type dredged up by typical structured interviews) but also unexpected information—insights or evidence offered voluntarily by the applicant. For example, a total of eight male and female applicants underwent a structured interview to select the top two candidates for a technical supervisor position. The top two candidates then were given nondirective interviews in order to make the final selection.

Why? First, the company wanted to treat both finalists in a gracious, nonregimented manner. One of them, after all, would soon be part of the managerial team. Second, interviewers were looking in this second interview for different data than those turned up in the structured interview. They wanted to assess the finalists' abilities to think on their feet, see implications and subtleties, generate ideas, show personal character, and so forth. A nondirective interview provided a better chance for these aspects of managerial competence to shine.

In nondirective interviewing, the interviewer begins with the assumption that a skilled applicant will guide conversation toward matters of mutual importance. If the interview doesn't "get there"—that is, focus on important issues—it's a good sign that the applicant is wrong for the job.

The process of nondirective interviewing, while quite free, is far from easy. The interviewer must listen carefully, not only to what the candidate is saying, but how he or she is approaching the topic, supporting major points, and using communication skills. All the while the interviewer must be an involved participant, not a spectator. The interviewee must sense that the interviewer cares about the conversation, wants to understand, and thinks deeply about the issues discussed. In the natural give-and-take of the nondirective interview, the interviewer occasionally must offer his or her own opinions.

But, as Walter Kiechel III warns in a recent issue of *Fortune*, nondirective interviewers have to "avoid two mistakes that most line managers make: doing all the talking yourself and straining so hard to come up with your next brilliant question that you neglect to listen to the candidate's response to the last one." Preparation, Kiechel says, is the key, "which means more than the customary 30 seconds looking over the candidate's resume while your secretary asks him if he wants coffee."

As a general rule of thumb, the higher the level of hiring or evaluation interview within the company, the more flexible and nondirective the interview will be.

A Typical Sequence of Interview Activities

Like a Frank Lloyd Wright architectural design, the "shape" of an interview depends upon what it hopes to accomplish. The following design, therefore, is intended as one possibility among many.

The Warm-up
As the candidate enters the interview room, the interviewer has already begun to establish rapport by bringing up some high interest/low threat topic, perhaps from the candidate's application. This is "small talk," but with an important purpose: the candidate should begin to feel free to open up to the interviewer. This stage of the

interview, while often fun both for the interviewer and interviewee, should consume no more than 10 percent of the total interview time.

Be especially cautious at the beginning of the interview, warns Fred Smith, sales manager of Quad Systems, of "shrewd applicants who will try to elicit information which will direct them to answer subsequent questions in a way they think you will like." Candidates may fish, for example, for "magic words" in your company culture— "cooperation," "team spirit," "creativity," and so forth. If at an interview you tip your hand early about your partyline words and slogans, you can expect to hear them over and over from the candidate through the interview.

The Contract
Without breaking the bond of friendliness and informality established in the warm-up, the interview makes a transition to the contract—a statement of what should take place during the interview. The contract statement, worded informally, should allow both parties to agree on the following:

- What we're here for
- The relative importance of the interview in the application process
- What information will be sought and how it will be used

Here is one contract statement.

As you know, Jack, we've invited you here to Apex corporate headquarters because we think you may have a great deal to offer as an accountant here. Our decision on your application will be based on this interview and your discussion later today with Marlene Phillips. In these next 30 minutes or so I want to understand as much as possible about your preparation, experience, and long term goals.

The Interview Body
These questions and responses take up about 80 percent of the interview time. Following a sequence of questions (in a structured interview) or a nondirective flow of conversation, the interviewer tries to obtain information and impressions called for by the interview objectives.

A subsidiary, but also important part, of the interview body is giving the applicant imformation about the company. Instead of launching into a canned speech, the interviewer can ask for and respond to the applicant's inquiries about

- Company history.
- Current projects.
- Policies and procedures.
- Job description.
- Opportunities for advancement.
- Method and time line for decision making on the application.
- Compensation and benefits.

The Wrap-up

The last 10 percent of the interview time is divided into three parts. First, the interviewer asks the interviewee if he or she has any questions not covered in the interview. Second, the interviewer briefly sums up what has been discussed. Finally, the interviewer expresses appreciation to the candidate and tells what the next step in the employment process will be. While an interviewer may sometimes hire good applicants on the spot, only rarely does he or she announce an unfavorable decision in the interview. Bad news may just prolong the interview and create unnecessary interpersonal tension.

STAGE SIX. TEST THE INTERVIEW PLAN

Your interview questions are now ready to roll out of the hangar— but will they fly?

Don't find out the hard way with real candidates. Take a bit of time to run through the interview sequence with a company employee (preferably one who holds or used to hold the job under consideration) playing the role of interviewee. As you run through the questions, decide for each

- Does it solicit the information we seek?
- Can it be misunderstood?
- Does it occur in the right place?
- Can the applicant's response be recorded?

By such testing, you'll also get a good feel for the length of the interview. You may have to trim or add questions to fit your allotted time.

STAGE SEVEN. TRAIN INTERVIEWERS TO USE THE INTERVIEW PLAN

Interviewers are the door by which new talent—or the lack thereof—comes into your business. Train them to understand

- The job description—what skills are we looking for?
- The interview objectives—what do we want to accomplish?
- The interview questions—why are we asking these questions?
- The interview record—how should responses be recorded and compared?
- The interview format—how structured or nondirective should the interview be?
- The interview sequence—in what order should questions be asked? How should interview time be distributed?

Especially with experienced interviewers, these training sessions need not be long or laborious. They can go far, however, to dismantling the "old boy system" of interviewing and hiring—the system based on intuitions, personalities, and often prejudice.

STAGE EIGHT. TRY THE INTERVIEW PLAN ON REAL APPLICANTS

This last stage involves careful monitoring and frequent communication among all interviewers involved in the process. The fine tuning, eliminating or rewriting poor questions and polishing good ones, continues throughout the life of the particular interview plan.

The personnel development firm of Pechner, Dorfman has taken this review process a step farther. Thirty days after hiring a candidate, the company requires him or her to fill out a carefully structured attitude survey measuring job satisfaction. If the employee's hiring interview misjudged his or her compatibility and satisfaction, interview questions are changed accordingly.

SPECIAL CONSIDERATIONS IN QUESTIONS
INVOLVING DRUGS

In accidents, absenteeism, and poor performance, drug abuse costs American industry well over $30 billion each year. Consequently, businesses have every reason to ask applicants about drug habits during the application process. (But see Chapter 9 for a discussion of such legally sensitive inquiries and how to handle them carefully.)

Interviewers can follow three guidelines in developing drug-related questions. First, phrase questions so that all value judgments, pro or con, are omitted. An applicant will certainly be unwilling to admit a "recreational" cocaine habit if the interviewer wears a "Prison for All Users!" button. On the other hand, a coy or flippant question about drugs may be misinterpreted by the applicant as a lax or encouraging drug climate in the company.

Second, use the drug vocabulary of the person being interviewed in all questions, even if it means using street names of drugs. In a classic case in New Jersey, an applicant for the position of shipping supervisor with a large trucking company was excluded from consideration because he answered "yes" to the interviewer's question, "Are you now using drugs?" As his court case showed, the applicant understood "drugs" to include a standard back-pain prescription from his physician.

Applicants may not understand questions such as "Are you using controlled substances?" or "Have you ever used hallucinogens?" For guidance on what to call commonly abused drugs, write to the Drug Enforcement Administration, Washington, D.C. for several pamphlets on substance abuse.

Finally, avoid absolutes in designing questions. In interviewing Frank, a 40-year-old midlevel manager, for example, do you really want to know "Have you ever used an illegal drug?" As applicants for positions from box clerk to Supreme Court Justice have discovered, such absolute questions invite either stigma or lying. Do you really care if Frank smoked grass at 17? If not, phrase your question accordingly: "Are you now using marijuana, cocaine, or any other controlled substance?"

Stanley Slowik, director of instructional systems for London House, Inc. (a psychological testing company), offers the following advice for employers: "You must balance your hiring needs against what you consider a tolerable level of employee behavior." He urges that, in reaching hiring decisions, employers consider when the behavior occurred, the applicant's age, the circumstances, and the type of substance abuse.

The Typical Corporate Selection Process

1. Manager initiates request for personnel (RFP).
2. Finance and senior management review and approve RFP.
3. RFP sent to Human Resources.
4. Human Resources adds job opening to all lists, internal and external, for open positions.
5. Human Resources checks RFP against internal transfer applicants.
6. Human Resources assembles an interview packet for interviewer(s), including position specifications, descriptions, and requirements).
7. Human Resources prescreens applicants and resumes.
8. Human Resources schedules interviews.
9. Human Resources interviews candidates.
10. Managers and supervisors interview candidates.
11. Managers and supervisors meet with Human Resources for candidate selection.
12. All references are checked for completeness and accuracy.
13. Offer is made.
14. Acceptance (in writing) forwarded to Human Resources where contracts, employee papers, and so forth, are prepared.
15. Human Resources notifies unsuccessful candidates.
16. Physical examination, if required.
17. Candidate begins work.
18. Human Resources completes record for hiring cycle, including how long it took from RFP to filling the position, number and types of applicants screened and interviewed, and reasons for decisions on candidates.

CHAPTER 9

INTERVIEWING AND
THE LAW

It's not hard to find outspoken critics of new laws impacting interviewing.

- "There's nothing legal left to ask!"
- "I'm afraid I'll get sued every time I turn down a minority applicant."
- "We don't even run employment ads anymore for fear of attracting problem applicants."

The purpose of this chapter will be to explain the intricacies and implications of current Title VII and EEOC legislation. While every effort has been made to verify the accuracy of the judgments expressed here, readers should seek specific legal advice from an attorney in matters related to actual interview questions and procedures.

THE INTENT OF THE NEW LAWS

Title VII and EEOC legislation all makes one point: the job selection process should be fair, unencumbered by prejudices. For example, a country that proclaims all human beings equal should not endure a system of hiring that, as the basis of selection, asks women how they plan to take care of their children during the day, but does not ask the question of men. Nor should dark skinned applicants automatically be screened from consideration because "they won't mix with our clientele."

Few Americans would disagree with the motives of such legislation. But putting the Fairness Doctrine into practice has required the reeducation of a whole generation of managers and interviewers. Questions that seemed innocuous a few years ago ("How old are you?" "Are you married?") now have landed many companies in court.

Smarting from expensive settlements and much negative publicity, companies now want every last interviewer in their employ to know what not to ask in the hiring process. The legal "hot spots" have grown from three or four in the 1970s to more than a dozen today.

Race or Color

The strict prohibition against hiring discrimination on the basis of race or color has several not-so-obvious corollaries. Prior to selection, candidates should not be asked to affix pictures of themselves to applications. Such pictures, of course, would tend to reveal race and/or color, and could be used to screen minority candidates out of contention for positions. (As noted below, the rules in such matters change somewhat once the candidate is hired.)

Similarly, an applicant (of any race or color) cannot legally be asked to state personal views on civil rights, to name his or her birthplace or that of relatives, or to list membership in organizations that may tend to reveal race or national origin. Birth certificates, naturalization papers, baptismal records and the like cannot be required prior to employment because they would tend to answer questions deemed illegal by EEOC or Title VII.

The matter of credit inquiries as part of the hiring process remains problematic. Federal law now prohibits an employer from basing hiring decisions on credit information of the sort that impacts blacks or other minorities as a class. For example, a relatively low economic status, few or no credit cards, and living arrangements with relatives can be expected among minorities historically disadvantaged in the American economic system. To use these facts as evidence of their unemployability is to compound and perpetuate a previous injustice.

Arrest records, too, tend to be higher among minority groups, and must be discounted on several grounds. First, the great majority of arrests never end in conviction; legally, the arrested person has not been proven guilty of a crime. Second, applicants with convictions should only be excluded from employment when the employer can show a direct relation between the convictions and the requirements of the job. A bank robber, for example, could be excluded from employment as a teller but perhaps not as a construction worker.

Many states, however, do provide for the employer's right to consider moral character and financial trustworthiness, including credit and conviction inquiries, for positions where such qualities are bona fide occupational requirements.

In an effort to do right by protected minority groups, some interviewers have stumbled into unexpected pitfalls, as an Ohio company discovered last year. Company interviewers, trained in what to ask and not to ask, nevertheless routinely noted "Black" or "Chicano" in the margins of the application materials and interview forms. These notes were intended, they said, as reminders to follow all applicable Title VII and EEOC regulations in interviewing these candidates. However, one minority applicant who was turned down for a job took the company to court for discrimination. Key evidence in his successful suit (at great expense to the company) was his employment papers, on which interviewers had scrawled notes pertaining to race.

Citizenship

As of May 1987, it became illegal for employers to consider citizenship in hiring decisions. But with the passage of Immigration Reform and Control Act in the same month, it is now also unlawful to hire or continue to employ unauthorized aliens knowingly.

What's an employer to do? A safe course is to ask applicants if they have the legal right to be employed in this country. An employer should not ask if the candidate is a citizen of another country (thereby revealing race or national origin), where they were born, or where their family lives. After the selection process, employers are now bound by the law to secure and examine documents establishing the identity of the candidate and his or her legal right to work in the U.S. If the candidate's pre-employment claims to legal work status prove bogus, the employer can terminate employment.

Family and Marital Status

Interviewers shouldn't inquire whether a candidate is single, married, divorced, or separated. Federal law interprets such questions as prejudicial to certain minority groups, such as women. Employers looking for wholesome, steady workers may make adverse judgments about a divorced woman, no matter what the individual circumstances. In some conservative communities, a mature man who is single could raise predjudicial or suspicious feelings in employers.

"But," employers object, "how am I supposed to hire a traveling sales manager if I can't ascertain what an applicant's responsibilities are to his kids and spouse?" The key is to pose all questions in relation to the job at hand, and to make questions equally applicable to both sexes. For example, an employer legally could ask "Are there any circumstances which could prevent you from traveling about ten days out of each month?" If the candidate answers "no," don't pursue the matter by asking "But don't you have children to take care of?" That question, unfortunately, is almost exclusively aimed at women—few employers would ask it of a man.

Often, illegal questions spring from the best of intentions. Companies, wanting to determine in advance how much it will cost to relocate a potential new employee, ask (illegally) "Do you own your own home?" and "Is your spouse employed?" These questions, according to the New York training firm Communispond, must be rephrased: "What circumstances, if any, would make relocation to our city difficult for you?"

What if an applicant volunteers personal information: "You see, I'm a divorced mother with three kids, and I really can't predict all the family emergencies that may come up from time to time and prevent me from making some trips." Just because the applicant volunteers information does not mean that it's fair game for the employer to use it in the selection process. When such information comes to court, it is difficult for an employer to prove how the information became part of the application file. All the court sees is its presence there, with strong implications of discrimination.

Therefore, in many companies interviewers are trained to respond to all volunteered but illegal information: "I understand, Ms. Covington, what you have volunteered to tell me about your family situation. I want you to know that this information is not being recorded as part of your application, nor will it be considered in any way as part of our hiring process." It's a mouthful to say, but it sets the record straight. The interviewer should communicate the message with courtesy so as not to make the candidate not feel he or she has done something illegal.

Sex and Sexual Preference

The list of jobs that legally are "for men only" or "for women only" is shorter and shorter each month. Men are hired to apply acrylic nails and women to frame houses. Courts consider all of the following questions to be sexually discriminatory:

• Inquiries regarding the original name of an applicant whose name has been changed by court order.
• Questions concerning child care, future plans for children, pregnancy, or status as principal wage earner in the family.
• Questions regarding the attitudes or biases of the applicant's spouse ("Will your husband object to you spending nights away in hotels?").
• Questions regarding the applicant's views on women's liberation issues.
• Inquiries about how long an applicant plans to work.

It may be both useful and legal for an employer to know if an applicant can keep work schedules, but that question should be asked directly rather than by implication as in the areas cited above.

Employers may not legally inquire about sexual preference, membership in organizations that may tend to reveal sexual preference, or attitudes toward homo- or heterosexual issues. If the candidate volunteers such information ("I want you to know from the outset that I'm gay"), it should not be recorded in the file or discussed as part of the application process.

Handicaps and Health-related Issues

The key for employers in this thorny area of questioning is to keep the cart behind the horse: job-related requirements should be described, and only then should the candidate be asked if he or she has any physical handicap, illness, or condition that might keep them from performing on the job. (These guidelines are spelled out in the Rehabilitation Act of 1973.)

Just the opposite occurs too often: employers begin by asking an applicant to describe physical handicaps and conditions. Then the employer goes on to discuss why the job at hand can't be done by a person with such limitations. The applicant cannot help feeling discriminated against, as hundreds of court cases attest. In such instances, the burden of proof falls on the employer to show that any purported physical or mental requirements for the job are, in fact, due to "business necessity" and safety.

Employers must be willing to make what the pertinent legislation calls "reasonable accommodation" to assist physically or mentally handicapped employees in the performance of job duties. Such accommodations include changing the physical structure of the workplace and providing necessary aids.

Catastrophic diseases such as cancer and AIDS pose particularly difficult dilemmas for employers. Applicants cannot be denied employment on the basis of the employer's "best guess" about their prognosis or longevity. Nor can an employer turn down an applicant because of rumored contagion (as in many AIDS cases), medical evidence to the contrary.

Age

In many job categories (including airline attendants, sales positions, and others) employers have opted for the under-30 applicant. He or she can often be hired for less and can be expected to serve the company for many years.

The Age Discrimination in Employment Act puts strict curbs on such age discrimination. Applicants now cannot be asked to state their age, except to determine if they meet legal age requirements in the state (usually 18 or 21). Questions that imply the age of the applicant ("When did you graduate from college?") are similarly prohibited.

As in the other "hot spots" above, the best guideline is to stick to job-related concerns. Define the job requirements according to what a person must do, not by what he or she is. Then hire based on performance requirements.

Religion

It is unlawful to screen applicants on the basis of religion (or lack thereof). Many candidates, to demonstrate their "solid citizen" status, volunteer information about church membership and service. Employers should not follow up such volunteered information with questions such as "Oh, who's your pastor?" or "Is Mike Bernstein a member of your synagogue?" Even when intended as idle chat, these questions may be interpreted by the applicant and the courts as an unlawful inquiry into issues having no bearing on the job.

Beyond gross religious discrimination ("No Catholics can work here," etc.) there lie more subtle and prevasive areas of prejudice. Many employers look upon some religions as "holiday happy," and reject applicants who will feel bound to take such religious days off. Other employers are looking for someone to work Saturdays and Sundays and therefore shy away from anyone who expresses a traditional religious commitment necessitating worship on those days.

In cases where the employer expects the employee to work on a religious holiday, including a weekly day of worship, the employer has the legal obligation to make reasonable scheduling adjustments to accommodate for the employee's religious practices.

Application Forms

Not without reason, interviewers often hesitate to generate questions on their own and retreat instead to the "fill-in-the-blank" questions contained on company application forms. Unfortunately, those forms in many cases have not been reviewed or changed in a number of years. If anything, the interviewee working from an application form is more likely, not less, to stumble into legal territory in the interview.

In a regular cycle, certainly at least once a month, companies should have their application forms reviewed by personnel professionals and legal staff. Federal and state laws affecting hiring change rapidly, and the stakes are high for compliance.

Employment Testing

In response to the apparent hazards of interviewing following Title VII and EEOC legislation, employers at first switched to "objective" written tests as a primary device for selecting from among job applicants. That practice, while certainly not illegal, no longer seems so attractive to suit-sensitive employers.

In a spate of selection discrimination cases, employers found themselves pressed by the courts to demonstrate the validity of the tests used as accurate measures of what it took to succeed in the jobs being considered. Well, employers argued at first, the tests were "professionally produced," meaning they were prepared by PhDs. Not relevant, said the courts. Next, employers endeavored to show that the knowledge, skills, and abilities assessed by the employment test did, in fact, coincide with knowledge, skills, and abilities used on the job. Still not directly relevant, said the courts.

So to the present: for a legally "safe" pre-employment test, an employer must be able to show that the test measures employee attributes central to successful job performance; that those attributes are measured and weighted in proportion to their importance on the job; and that the level of difficulty of the test fairly reflects the level of difficulty of the job.

That's a tall order, and too expensive or legally perilous for many companies. But others, says management consultant Robert J. Solomon, are finding ways to hire better through legal tests. The key, he points out, is for companies to "analyze a job to identify the performance issues they want to test for. Next they should choose selection procedures that are objective and as nearly as possible simulate the actual job." Examples of such companies are numerous and growing.

• Commonwealth Edison in Chicago has used an honesty test for twelve years as part of its job application process for some divisions.
• ABC, General Motors, and IBM screen job candidates for drug use, and many large corporations are now studying the legal and social wisdom of screening for AIDS.
• London House, a producer and distributor of business tests in Park Ridge, Illinois, has sold more than $6 million in tests, most of them honesty tests, to food service companies, banks, jewelry stores, supermarkets, and other retailers. One of these, the Transit Operators Selection Inventory, has been used by more than 100 transportation authorities in their hiring. The test claims to measure not only for experience, background, skills, and abilities, but also the applicant's emotional health, potential for drug use, and tendency toward violent behavior.
• Xerox Corporation's computer services division in Los Angeles made use of a computer-analyzed handwriting test produced by Handwriting Research Corporation in Phoenix to rate telemarketing personnel. According to Ron Bell, a Xerox sales manager, "the accuracy rate was 100 percent; the high scorers were our superstars, and the low scorers are no longer with us."

Some companies have been encouraged in the use of IQ tests as predictors of employee success. Professor John E. Hunter of Michigan

State has found a high correlation between IQ scores and performance on the job.

Many banks and retailers now use polygraph (lie detector) tests to check employee attitudes toward stealing and past involvement in theft experiences. But the "science" of lie detecting is still more of an art, says Robert LoPresto, former head of personnel at Fairchild and Levi Strauss: "There's little evidence they are accurate, and you could open yourself to lawsuits."

The Construction of a Valid Test

As reported in *Personnel Journal*, February 1987, "the bulk of recent court decisions involving pre-employment testing support the Equal Employment Opportunity Commission's guidelines for 'good' tests. Every employer needs to know how to recognize, if not generate, such tests."

1. Valid tests grow out of a careful analysis of the tasks and skills necessary to performance of a particular job.
2. Test items are based on those tasks and skills and should be constructed so as to require problem-solving abilities and critical thinking from applicants rather than mere memorization.
3. Prototypical tests should be conducted and evaluated using real workers in the job situation.
4. Based on the results of such preliminary testing, a statistical item analysis should be performed to determine the accuracy of the test in differentiating between good and poor performers.
5. Finally, the test should be revised by content and test construction experts so that each item is relevant to job performance and is appropriate in level of difficulty.

The economics of meaningful testing can be attractive, as Raymond M. Berger and Donna H. Tucker calculate: "Imagine that a company is recruiting 20 management trainees and uses a test to select the trainees. The test has improved the company's selection accuracy by 25 percent and the salary of the trainee is $15,000 per year; the cost of the testing program is $2,000. Gross savings in selection: 25 percent times 20 trainees times $15,000 per trainee equals $75,000. After subtracting the $2,000 cost of testing, the company realizes a net savings of $73,000."

State Laws

Employers must be aware that many states have legislation impacting hiring. Some outlaw the use of polygraph tests in selection procedures; others prohibit discrimination based on the applicant's attainment of a General Education Development certificate instead of a high school diploma.

In Illinois, a dishonorable discharge from military service cannot be used as a reason for not hiring an applicant. The District of Columbia bars discrimination on the basis of "sexual orientation, family responsibilities, physical handicap, or political affiliation." (Georgetown University recently ran afoul of this law when it refused to recognize a gay student group as a legitimate organization on its campus.)

How a Disgruntled Applicant Proves Discrimination

A plaintiff claiming discrimination must demonstrate that he or she

- belongs to a class protected by relevant legislation
- is qualified for the job.
- was rejected in favor of someone not a member of a protected class.
- was rejected for a job that has gone unfilled.

Faced with this complaint, an employer then has a chance to justify the hiring decision. The plaintiff can challenge that explanation, drawing in any evidence, written or oral from the interview and selection process, that might tend to prove discrimination.

As reported in *Nation's Business,* June 1985, the stakes can be high. "In addition to legal expenses, an employer losing a suit could face a court order to hire the plaintiff, pay all accumulated back wages, and—where willful discrimination because of age is proved—pay double damages."

SUMMING UP

Like ripples circling out from a stone thrown into a pond, the implications of Title VII and EEOC legislation continue to challenge managers and interviewers. Amendments and new laws affecting selection procedures appear every few weeks. Employers, therefore, are well advised to

• keep in touch with legal counsel on hiring procedures.
• read widely in journals and magazines such as *Personnel, Personnel Journal, Fortune, Forbes* and *Personnel Administrator*.
• most important, develop company-wide programs that meet the intent of Title VII and EEOC regulations in a proactive way, rather than reacting to complaints and lawsuits.

Legal and Illegal Questions

Religion

Legal to Ask

Virtually all questions regarding religion should be avoided.

Illegal to Ask

Can you work on Sundays? What is your religion? What religious holidays will you require off?

Age

Legal to Ask

Are you between the ages of 40 and 70? If not, please give your age?

Illegal to Ask

When were you born? How old are you? Aren't you a bit old for this job?

Citizenship

Legal to Ask

Do you have a legal right to be employed in the U.S.?

Illegal to Ask

Are your parents, husband, or wife native-born or naturalized citizens of this country? Are you a native-born citizen? What country are you a citizen of?

Relations

Legal to Ask

Do you have any relatives already employed in this company?

Illegal to Ask

What is the name and address of your spouse? What are the names and addresses of your children? What type of work does your spouse, mother, or father do?

Linguistic Background

Legal to Ask

What languages can you write and/or speak fluently?

Illegal to Ask

Is English your second language? What is your native language? How did you learn to speak a second or third language?

Arrest Record

Legal to Ask

Do you have a valid driver's license? Have you been convicted of a crime? If so, when?

Illegal to Ask

Have you ever been arrested? What were the circumstances? What was the outcome?

Social Involvement

Legal to Ask

If you think your membership in certain organizations is relevant to this job, list those organizations.

Illegal to Ask

List all social organizations, and societies to which you belong.

Marital Status

Legal to Ask

Avoid all questions related to marital status.

Illegal to Ask

Are you married? Do you have or plan to have children? What does your spouse do? What plans have you made for child care? How does your spouse feel about you being gone on business trips? How much is your total family income? What health coverage do you now have through your spouse? Do you favor family planning and birth control?

CHAPTER 10

PROBING, CONTROLLING, AND CONCLUDING

The interview should not devolve into a lecture, with you "taking notes" on the speeches of the applicant. Prevent the lecture syndrome by effective probes. These are short, direct questions that usually follow up on a longer question or on some aspect of the applicant's response.

The Challenge Probe

You can test the applicant's ability to deal constructively with criticism by a challenge probe. This inquiry, sometimes called the "devil's advocate" question, challenges the truth, completeness, or relevance of the applicant's response. Note that the interviewer does not blatantly claim that the interviewee is wrong—instead the challenge probe raises the question of another side to the story.

APPLICANT:

Managing others means really listening to their concerns. The best manager I ever had took time to make friends with her employees.

INTERVIEWER using Challenge Probe:

Do you see any hazards involved when managers try to befriend employees?

This probe extends the line of questioning to determine how the applicant responds when challenged. Will he bristle? Will he

133

completely "change his tune"? Will he fall silent? Any or all of these responses can provide extremely valuable data when it comes time to decide among candidates for the job.

Sample Challenge Probes

- Many people at this company would disagree with that statement.
- Isn't there another side to that story?
- What would you say if I told you I completely disagreed?
- Some of the best people we've interviewed have just taken the opposite point of view.

The Amplification/Clarification Probe

This mode of questioning seeks to develop an applicant's response more fully. The interviewer must be careful to let the applicant fill in the missing pieces. Especially in interviews where good rapport has been established, it is often tempting for the interviewer to "help" the applicant by suggesting what could or should be said.

APPLICANT:

At Acme, my major job responsibility was to keep other employees in line.

INTERVIEWER, probing for amplification and clarification:

Keeping other employees in line?

Note that by saying the cryptic phrase back to the applicant, the interviewer doesn't give away any desired answers—as might happen if the interviewer had said, "Do you mean in areas of discipline?"

Sample Amplification/Clarification Probes

- What do you mean?
- Why do you say that?
- How would you support that opinion?
- Tell me more about . . .
- In other words, you're saying that . . .
- I'm confused about one point. You said that . . .

The Conclusionary Probe

Conclusionary probes are used throughout the interview, not just at the end. They test whether the applicant can come to a final point. Bright, decisive candidates can come to conclusions; weaker applicants will let their responses wander back to old territory or on to new topics without coming to conclusions.

APPLICANT:

> . . . and I had other summer jobs along the same line. Most of them were really quite enjoyable.

INTERVIEWER, using a conclusionary probe:

> Overall, what did your summer experiences teach you?

In this probe, the interviewer tests whether the candidate can draw several minutes of discussion—in this case, on summer jobs—to a single point. If the candidate succeeds, the interviewer will give high marks for intelligence and the power to generalize from specific experience. If the candidate stumbles awkwardly or continues to tell more stories about summer jobs, the interviewer will give low marks.

Sample Conclusionary Probes

- What does this all add up to?
- What for you is the bottom line?
- Even if we talked about this topic for the next hour, what would be the basic message?
- What conclusion(s) did you draw from those experiences?
- What does that all mean to you?

The Investigative Probe

In a hiring environment where "white lies" are said to occur on as many as 80 percent of resumes, interviewers must be able to probe beneath the applicant's surface assertions. This line of questioning must be done in such a way as to not insult the candidate or arouse hostility. The interviewer's suspicions, after all, may be unfounded. In that case, a good candidate could inadvertently be lost by insensitive questioning. And even when the interviewer's suspicions are well-founded, direct accusations only cause the candidate to "stone-wall." Proper investigative probes open doors to dark areas cautiously.

APPLICANT:

> But the company had budget problems and had to make a few career adjustments, including mine.

INTERVIEWER, using an investigative probe:

> The reason you lost your last job was because of the company's financial problems?

In this case, the interviewer senses that something is being hidden in the candidate's use of the euphemism "career adjustments." To get at the truth, the investigative probe restates the applicant's assertion in plain, unmistakable terms. The candidate may say "yes" or "no"—or offer a more complete, and perhaps more honest, explanation.

Sample Investigative Probes

- Tell me again exactly what your job responsibilities were.
- Are the dates of your employment on your resume rough estimates?
- If we contact your former employer, will she have the same view of the incident you described?
- Does the overall GPA you've given fairly reflect your work in your major courses?
- Is there anyone I can call to verify that?
- How would you support that point if we asked you to?

Through effective probes, a skilled interviewer can turn a stiff, "canned" interview into an open, revealing conversation. "I always remember the Wizard of Oz," says one Washington interviewer. "Behind the air of confidence and the big voice is a very different person—often more interesting and more likable than the pretentious facade. I try to probe until that person comes out from behind the curtain."

CONTROLLING TOPICS AND MAKING TRANSITIONS

Mary Connors, an MBA student, just completed two back-to-back interviews.

> The difference between the two was enormous but difficult to describe. In the first, I felt like a TV set. The interviewer kept switching channels and out came a minute or two of whatever was on my mind for that topic. But the other was much more interesting. The interviewer let me take the lead in conversation from time to time. The whole process was much less regimented and jerky. Instead of feeling like a TV set, I felt more like an actress in a live drama.

Maintaining Control

Inexperienced interviewers, fearful that the applicant will seize control of the interview, maintain control by asking a question, listening to the answer, making notes, then asking another question, and so forth for half an hour or more. The disadvantages to this "I pitch— you catch" approach to interviewing are many.

- Applicants feel distant from the interviewer and therefore may withhold sincere thoughts and feelings. Answers will tend to be "canned" and rehearsed.
- Interviewers have difficulty following up on a particular response. Instead, they're off to a new question on the list.
- Applicants receive a cold, aloof impression of the company. The interview comes to feel more like an interrogation than an expression of the company's interest in their application.
- Interviewers lose personal warmth and rapport. When they give up the ordinary skills of conversation, interviewers become more like automatons in their speech patterns and judgments.

For all these reasons, interviewers should be encouraged to engage applicants in lively, natural conversation. The interview, for both interviewer and interviewee, should be both interesting and enjoyable.

Does "lively, natural conversation" mean that control of topics and time limits are out of the interviewer's control? Not at all. By practicing the six techniques below, interviewers can give conversation and a line of questioning precisely where they want it to go without appearing brusque or detached.

Controlling the Sequence of Topics

Use a keyword to make a transition to the next question.

INTERVIEWER:

> Jill, you used the word 'loyalty' in what you just told me. What does loyalty to a company mean to you?

Put an undesirable topic on "hold," substituting the topic you wish.

INTERVIEWER:

> You raised the issue of compensation, Bob, and we definitely will want to discuss that a bit later. First, though, let me ask you . . .

Take a moment to tell how one question relates to the next.

INTERVIEWER:

> Well, so far we have discussed your skills as an individual. Now let's talk about you as a member of a team.

Controlling Length of Responses

Cut off overly long answers by a complimentary reference to the applicant's thoroughness.

INTERVIEWER:

> Let me interrupt, Bill. You've given me a very thorough picture of your undergrad days. Now I want to ask you . . .

Indicate the approximate length of response you desire.

INTERVIEWER:

> I know we could discuss this matter for an hour—but, in just a sentence or two, tell me why you would be a good manager.

Indicate the relative importance of your question as a guideline for the desired length of response.

INTERVIEWER:

> One of the most important questions we ask all candidates is, Where do you want to be within this company in three years?

(or)

INTERVIEWER:

> This is really a side question, Bob, but tell me, why did you change majors from anthropology to accounting?

With experience in using these techniques, interviewers won't have to worry about, on the one hand, the "runaway" interview or, on the other hand, a dictatorial and uninteresting interviewing manner.

Dealing with Resistance

"How do I get them to talk?" complained one company interviewer after a rather unsuccessful series of interviews at a a state university. "I ask the standard questions, they just won't open up. I get a sentence or two, and then an embarrassed silence."

Interviewees at all levels of experience can become tongue-tied in certain interviewing environments. It's important to understand the forces that make people unwilling or unable to express themselves.

Applicants clam up when they feel threatened.
A particularly austere look from the interviewer, a harsh or judgmental question early in the interview, an unexpected flood of jargon or technical terms—all these can cause interviewees to feel threatened. Suggested solution: spend more time in nonthreatening, getting-to-know you talk at the beginning of the interview. Refer to the resume or application form to come up with sports, social, recreational, or cultural interests that the candidate can talk about freely and enjoyably.

Applicants tend to reflect back the behavior
of the interviewer.
If the interviewer is tense, terse, and blunt in questioning, the interviewee will tend to mimick those same behaviors. This monitoring effect often produces short and inadequate responses. The appli-

cant, in entering the world of the interviewer, consciously or subconsciously tries to follow the leader. It's a case of "when in Rome, do as the Romans." Suggested solution: tape record or videotape a few of your interviews. During the playback, pay attention to your social style. Do your questions and comments model the kind of natural, sincere expression you want from the interviewee? If not, change!

Applicants may be too self-conscious and self-judgmental.

Like the whine of a loudspeaker too close to a microphone, a feedback problem occurs when an applicant simultaneously tries to talk to you while evaluating each word he or she says. Symptoms of such a problem are frequent start-overs, run-on or broken sentences, and outright expressions of frustration: "I'm just not saying it right." Suggested solution: Support the early, nervous responses of the applicant with overt signs of acceptance and, if possible, approval.   A simple smile—not a sarcastic one—in reaction to an applicant's response can do much to make conversation flow much more freely.

Dealing with Hostility

"If they want a job here, they'd better not give me any lip." That attitude on the part of interviewer often guarantees that strong-willed, independent, dynamic applicants won't be employed by the company.

Some interviewers, in fact, interpret an applicant's honest and straightforward expressions of feeling as resistance or hostility, as in the following transcript:

INTERVIEWER:

Let's see, you live in Glenview. You made a long drive to get here.

APPLICANT:

About 35 miles.

The interviewer reacts negatively to this simple comment. He had expected this applicant, like most, to make a joke of the drive: "The curse of the working class." The unexpected answer peeves him. "What, does he think he's some kind of a hero for commuting 35 miles? I do it every day!"

Clearly, there is no place as an interviewer for individuals so insecure and thin-skinned as to be put off by blunt, honest answers. Before deciding how to deal with hostility, every interviewer must first determine if, in fact, hostility is present.

One good test is the "fact vs. feeling" test. When an interviewer feels that an applicant's look or comment has hostile intent, it's wise to separate fact—what the applicant actually did or said—from feeling, that is, the response felt by the interviewer. Upon such examination, many interviewers discover that applicants in reality did nothing hostile at all.

For example, is an applicant's straightforward, respectful expression of disagreement a hostile act? Not at all. If an interviewer bristles at being challenged, he or she must not blame the applicant for the hostility. If anything, the applicant may simply be showing deep interest in the issues being discussed.

When hostility is, in fact, present, it usually comes from one of three causes:

The applicant has been disappointed.
People often decide they have nothing to lose after receiving bad news—such as "we don't think this job is for you." They strike out verbally in anger. For this reason, try to avoid indicating your decision on the applicant during the interview itself.

The applicant feels insulted.
When challenged about the accuracy of an employment date on the resume, when asked to clarify a vague, wordy response, when quizzed closely about actual past employment responsibilities, some applicants decide their integrity is being questioned. Tempers flare. Avoid taking the heat at such moments by wording your questions in a way that does not attack pride or self-worth.

Not: "Haven't you inflated your job description quite a bit?"

Instead: "In addition to what you have stated on your resume, tell me specifically what you did on a typical day in your last job."

A helpful guideline here is to remember that, as an interviewer, it is your function to understand and evaluate the applicant, not to point out the error of his or her ways. The latter career is reserved for preachers.

The applicant thinks that you value an abrasive,
hard-hitting approach.

Some applicants come to the interview expecting to fight fire with
fire—to show they're "tough" and "can't be pushed around." This
chip-on-the-shoulder attitude can be defused by direct confrontation,
as in the following transcript.

INTERVIEWEE (with a sneer):

> I didn't come here to defend myself. Tell me what you have to
> offer.

INTERVIEWER (amicably):

> You seem to be feeling some anger or hostility that I'm not feeling.
> Did my question strike you wrong?

INTERVIEWEE (Calming down):

> I'm used to being more of a hammer than a nail, I guess.

INTERVIEWER:

> That's one of the reasons we're interested in you.

Note this brief transcript that the interviewer did not have to
apologize, explain, or withdraw his line of questioning. The break-
through occurred when he focused on the hostility and looked for its
cause in a open, nonjudgmental way.

CONCLUDING THE
INTERVIEW AND
FOLLOWING UP

Like old Bugs Bunny cartoons, too many interviews end with an
abrupt, "That's all, folks!" Such interviews quit, not end.

At Countrywide Credit Industries, vice president Tom Boone
makes a practice of reserving the last 20 percent of the interview
time for conclusionary remarks. "I find that most of the important
points come out when I let a candidate know the interview is winding
up. It's his or her last chance to put their best foot forward."

Conclusionary Signals.

You can indicate that the interview is approaching its conclusion without stifling further conversation. Consider using any of the following signals (if the interview has an assigned time limit).

- I'd like to pursue that point with you, Jack, but our time is getting away from us. Let's use our last ten minutes or so to—
- Let me stop you for a minute, Barbara. We have about five minutes left and I want to make sure you've had a chance to ask any final questions or express concerns about this position.
- I've enjoyed talking with you. We have about ten minutes left. What do you think we should talk about in the remaining time?

If the interview has no specific time limit, use one of these signals:

- We've covered a lot of ground in our conversation. Let's wind up picturing you in this position.
- I only have two questions left for you, Jeff, and then you probably have some for me.

What Is Included in a Conclusion?

Your last 20 percent or so of the interview time provides a critical opportunity to

- summarize what has passed so far in the interview. The interviewer may want to sum up what the company has to offer, and then ask the applicant to sum up his or her major strengths.
- provide an opportunity for the applicant's questions. A strong applicant will usually not have left a great many questions or major concerns other than the compensation/benefit issues for the very end of the interview. Be prepared, however, to give specific answers about money in response to direct questions. The old prohibition for applicants against discussing money is fading rapidly. Modern interviewees want to discuss compensation openly.
- plant final thoughts and impressions. Studies show that both what you say and how you say it in conclusion will remain with the

applicant longer than any other words during the interview. Plan to project sincere interest, real appreciation, and interpersonal warmth during final minutes with candidates you want to hire.

• establish follow-up expectations and agendas. What can the applicant expect following the interview? Tell him or her. Do you want the applicant to provide you with further materials, attend other interviews, and so forth? If so, make sure your mutual agenda is clearly understood. If it involves dates, office numbers, and deadlines, you should write it down for both your sakes.

What to Do Once the Interview Is Over

You've shaken the applicant's hand, the interview is ended, and you are once more in the relative quiet of your own office. Before the next interview or interruption, take a few moments to

• complete whatever notes, scoresheet, or evaluation form you've decided to use as part of your decision-making process. Your impressions may change upon later reflection, but they will never be as fresh as immediately after the interview. Get down the data you will need for the later decisions. In the case of protected applicants (minorities, the handicapped, senior citizens, and so forth) remember that you may have to show objective reasons why you didn't choose to hire as well as why you did. Thorough notes can keep the company out of expensive legal problems.

• set in motion any follow-up letters, inquiries, phone calls or other communications arising out of the interview. If, for example, you want to send a short thank-you note to the applicant, dictate it or set your secretary to the task. If certain representations made during the interview have to be checked out, assign the task right away or make plans to do it yourself. These are the small but important details of the interview process that otherwise often fall through the cracks. "At Interstate Bank," says Bob Bradley, vice president in charge of training, "we provide interviewers with 30 minutes follow-up time for every hour they spend on interviews. This period gives us a much better chance of getting accurate, timely feedback and keeping complete records."

• reassemble all application materials. The candidate's file has probably been discombobulated on your desk. Put it back in order, together with any new materials the candidate has left with you. Send

it immediately back to filing. Personnel folders have a well-known reputation for getting lost "somewhere" in the boss's office.
• let other levels of interviewers know your interview has taken place. In most companies, separate interviewers wisely withhold their opinions from one another until all interviews have been completed. But the ever-threatening chaos of the business day can be forestalled by a brief phone call or memo: "Brad, I met with the candidate this morning. She's available for your interview any time after 1 P.M."
• take a short relaxation break if another interview is to follow immediately. One-on-one, eye-to-eye interviewing is hard work. Give yourself a few moments to relax in preparation for another eager, intense applicant. Interviewers who fail to prevent "burnout" in this way tend to favor early applicants and to reject later candidates— those interviewed in the bleary last sessions of the day.

HANDBOOK OF INTERVIEW TYPES

THE SELECTION INTERVIEW

By far the most common type of interview in American business, the selection interview places those who know the company best in direct contact with those who want to join the company. The selection interview has traditionally been one-on-one, for periods ranging from 15 minutes to an hour or more. In the 1980s, more and more companies are using group interviews, with several interviewers to one applicant, as a way of speeding up and giving more validity to the interview process.

Goals

• To collect data, through questioning and discussion, that can be used to choose the best employees available. Such data includes evidence of the candidate's intelligence, aptitude, attitudes, personality, habits, activities, interests, education, background, work history, integrity, communication skills, and personal/professional goals.
• To communicate important information about the company to the candidate.

Common Problems

• Interviewers talk too much. Applicants, because they are the primary information source for your decision making, should do approximately 80 percent of the talking during the interview.
• Interviewers ask the wrong questions. Many applicants come prepared with "canned" answers regarding their education, career goals, work history, and so forth. Interviewers must ask questions (like those below) that test the applicant's ability to think quickly, express clearly, and get to the point.
• Applicants mumble and stumble due to nerves. Often the brightest applicants suffer most from nervous tension, perhaps because they are so motivated to perform well. At the beginning of the interview,

skilled interviewers take 10 to 15 percent of the interview time to put the candidate at ease through small talk.

• Interviewers do not record data for later decision making. For legal reasons and effective selection procedures, interviewers must make notes on what the applicant said, how he or she appeared, and how well he or she communicated.

Sample Questions

Work History

1. Please tell me about your previous job.
2. What do you believe were your major responsibilities in that job?
3. What kind of job experiences have you had that relate to this position?
4. What aspects of your previous job did you like?
5. What aspects of your previous job did you dislike?
6. What are some of the things you spent the most time on in your previous job? How much time did you spend on each?
7. What are some of the assignments in your previous job that you did particularly well? Why?
8. What are some of the assignments in your previous job that you found difficult to do? Why?
9. Tell me about a problem you solved on your previous job.
10. What did you do when you couldn't solve a problem on your job?
11. Describe your boss's method of management. Evaluate your boss.
12. For what things did your boss compliment you?
13. In your previous job, how much work was done on your own? As part of a team?
14. What was the most innovative idea you introduced in your previous job?
15. Describe your techniques for getting the job done.

Personal Background, Attitudes, and Goals

1. What schooling have you had that can be helpful in performing this job?

⌐wn objectives with regard to this position?

⌐term career objectives?

⌐ere do you want to be one (three, five)

⌐?

⌐n to do to reach your career objectives?

⌐l about the progress you've made so far in

⌐ previous job?

⌐e your talents and abilities are well-matched

⌐ow and why?

⌐r greatest assets?

9. ⌐⌐   ⌐ choose the school you attended?
10. Did you change your course of study? Why?
11. Did you change schools? Why?
12. Why did you major in your particular field?
13. In what extracurricular activities were you involved in school?
14. What made you choose those particular activities?
15. What acomplishments did you feel proud of at school?
16. What experiences at school do you wish you had a chance to do over? Why?
17. How did you pay for your education?
18. Did you hold any leadership positions in school?
19. What things interest you outside of work?
20. What do you like to do best?
21. What things give you the greatest satisfaction?
22. Have your interests changed in recent years?
23. How well did you do in school?
24. What grades did you receive?
25. In what courses did you do best?
26. With what courses did you have the most trouble?
27. From what courses did you get the most benefit? Why?
28. From what courses did you get the least benefit? Why?
29. Do you feel your grades fairly reflect your ability? If not, why?
30. If you had it to do over again, would you have taken the same course of study? Why?
31. How do you view the job for which you are now applying?
32. If you were to obtain this job, in what areas could you contribute immediately? Where would you need training?

33. What barriers do you see that might prevent you from performing your job as effectively as you would like to?
34. Do you have the tools and support that you need to do your job?
35. What do you understand to be the mission or purpose of the company?
36. How do you feel about the day-to-day tasks involved with this position?
37. How well do you work under pressure? Give me some examples.
38. How well do you get along with your peers?
39. What kind of people rub you the wrong way?
40. How do you go about motivating other people?
41. What kinds of problems do you enjoy solving?
42. What can you tell me about your level of ambition?
43. How do you spend your free time?
44. What newspapers and magazines do you read regularly?
45. What is your definition of success?
46. What did you learn from your previous position?
47. What can you tell me about your level of creativity?
48. Do you work better alone or as part of a team? Explain.
49. What motivates you?
50. Why should this company hire you?

Sample Application for Employment

This form has been designed to elicit a significant sample of the applicant's writing—a good measure of thinking skills, education, and managerial potential. The form is intended as a guideline and should be altered to serve your particular selection needs and approved by your legal counsel.

Statement of Equal Opportunity: This company is an Equal Opportunity Employer and does not take into consideration age, sex, national origin, race, color, religion, or non-job-related handicaps in its hiring process or employment decisions.

Your full name _____
                  Last   First   Middle

Address, including ZIP:_____

Social Security Number:_____

Phone Number: ( ) _____

Hours when you can be reached by telephone: _____

What position are you applying for?

Are you applying for full- or part-time work? Please indicate the days and hours you will be available to work.

This company abides by the legal age limits on employment. Are you as old or older than the legal minimum age of ____ for employment? ( )yes ( ) no Have you passed the legal mandatory age of ____ for retirement? ( ) yes ( ) no How did you come to know about this company and possible job openings here?

Do we now have an application on file for you from a previous application here? If so, give details.

List all family members other than a spouse now working at this company:

Please list and explain any convictions for felonies. (Do not list or explain arrests that did not lead to conviction.)

Please explain any personal conditions (physical, mental or medical) that may pose a problem for you in carrying out the job for which you are applying.

Do you have a legal right to work in the United States? (If selected for employment, you may be asked to provide proof of citizenship or alien registration status.)

Describe your writing, speaking, and reading skills for any languages you possess. Include your primary language.

If you belong to social or business organizations that, in your opinion, relate to the job for which you are applying, list those organizations.

If you are involved in activities or have interests that, in your opinion, relate to the job for which you are applying, describe those activities and interests.

Summary of Past Employment

Please list, from most to least recent, company names of your past employers. (After filling out the blanks below, use the same format on separate paper for all positions.)

Company Name and Type of Business: —————————

Address: —————————

Phone: —————————

Dates of Employment: —————————

Manager's Name: —————————

Your Job Title: —————————

Responsibilities: _____

Salary History: _____

Reason(s) for Leaving: _____

Summary of Education and Training

College(s) attended: _____

Number of years completed: _____

Degrees received: _____

Describe how your college experiences relate to the job for which you are applying. Include any extracurricular activities or interests you feel should be considered as part of your application.

Training or technical schools attended: _____

Number of years completed: _____

Major areas of study: _____

Certificates, licenses, or other recognition received:

Describe how your training experiences relate to the job for which you are applying. Include any extracurricular activities or interests you feel should be considered as part of your application.

High school(s) attended: _____

Number of years completed: _____

Diploma or certificate received: _____

(Please fill out the following only if no college or training experience has been listed.) Describe how your high school experiences relate to the job for which you are applying. Include any extracurricular activities or interests you feel should be considered as part of your application.

Summary of Skills

Describe your special skills, aptitudes, abilities, or other qualifications for the position you have applied for.

References

Please list at least three persons we may contact in reference to your application. Do not include past or present employers listed above under "Employment."

Reference Name	Address	Phone Number
1.		
2.		
3.		

Summary of Legal Notices

(Include here any special notices required in your city or state for certain protected classes of workers, including affirmative action notices regarding age, veteran status, handicap, race, and other areas of recent legislation. Consult appropriate government authorities and/or legal counsel to make sure the wording of such notices fits your company, your needs, and the law.)

Applicant's certification:

I certify that to the best of my knowledge the above statements, made willingly by me, are correct. It is agreed that any false statements made as part of this application may result in termination of my employment. It is further agreed that, if I am hired, my photograph may be taken for identification purposes.

_____

(signature)

Releases

By my initials in the appropriate spaces below, I indicate any and all releases given by me in relation to this application.

The company can contact schools listed for release of my educational or training record. Initial one: ( )yes ( )no

The company can contact my present employer with regard to information given in this application. Initial one: ( )yes ( )no

FIGURE H–1
Interview Appraisal Form

Name _____ School _____ Phone Number _____

Campus Address _____

Post Graduation _____

Mailing Address _____ Phone Number _____

Availability _____ Geographical Career

Date _____ Preference _____ Interests _____ G.P.A. _____

Selection Standard	Observations	Exceeds	Meets	Does Not Meet
	Relates to selection standards and to information reported by applicant or			
Presentation	Forcefulness, Organization, Conciseness—ask related questions.			
Achievements	Academic, Technical, Professional Contributions to previous employers. Do they relate to our needs?			
Ambitions	Career Goals, Financial Goals—are they realistic?			
Contributions	Long- and short-term, what can the candidate add to the organization?			
Is Candidate Sold on Pizza Hut	Understands Career Opportunity.			
Overall Reaction				

_____
Recruiter's Signature

Highly Recommended _____
Recommended _____
Reject _____

Source: Courtesy of Pizza Hut.

THE PERFORMANCE APPRAISAL INTERVIEW

Performance appraisals are often conducted informally, as when a group of managers meet to discuss the performance of their employees. Or performance appraisals can be formal, with set dates, cycles, and written appraisal instruments. In either case, the results of performance appraisals affect what matters most to employees: promotions, pay increases, relative power in the organization, transfers, and even terminations. Not surprisingly, the actions of employers in these areas have been rather thoroughly limited by Federal and state laws.

The import of these laws, as contained in the *Uniform Guidelines for Employee Selection Procedures* (U.S. Government Printing Office, 1978), are as follows:

1. Make sure the criteria by which you are evaluating employees are in fact important to successful performance of the job. If the ability to write well, for example, does not affect job performance, it should not be used as an evaluation criterion.

2. Build those criteria directly into a rating instrument so that your judgments are based upon success factors, not arbitrary opinion.

3. Take care to communicate your standards for performance to employees. This communication should be written as well as oral. Employers are wise to devise a "signoff" procedure to demonstrate that employees have read and understood the performance standards.

4. Train all evaluators, including supervisors and managers, in the use of any instruments or feedback forms used for evaluation. These instructions should be written and training procedures should be thorough enough to produce competent evaluators. The employer should be able to demonstrate a means of quality review and quality control on the evaluation process.

5. Document all evaluations, including your reasons for action taken. When challenged in court, employers usually must produce written evidence showing the basis on which the employee was evaluated and the method by which results were determined.

6. Oversee the evaluation process, making sure that changing job conditions are reflected in accompanying changes in the evaluation process.

Common Problems

• Employees perceive questions as disciplinary in nature. Especially when questions involve task performance, superior-subordinate relations, or time allocation, employees often feel that they are being criticized rather than evaluated. As a result, their answers are defensive and often somewhat hostile. Interviewers must make clear that, far from imposing criticism, they want to know the employee's thoughts and feelings about work situations.

• Employees look upon the process as unfair. Because they do not know or have not been informed of the standards by which they are being evaluated, employees often think of performance appraisals as "personality contests" or opportunities to flatter the boss. Going in to the performance appraisal, the employee should know a) what will be discussed, b) why those topics matter for job performance, and c) what will be done with the information given in the interview.

• Interviewers fail to refer to specific facts and to ask specific questions. In such an interview environment, employees can come to feel a free-floating sense of guilt and dread, somewhat akin to "Original Sin." The interviewer hints that "something" isn't quite right, but never puts a finger on the precise project, report, or manager at issue. As a consequence, the employee cannot respond specifically and factually.

• Interviewers convey dislike or disapproval for the employee, not the employee's behavior. If interviewers want to understand and evaluate the actions of employees, they must keep the focus of the interview steadily on those actions instead of on more diffuse topics such as personality. Employees can often provide meaningful explanations of particular actions they took. It's almost impossible, by contrast, to explain why they are who they are.

Sample Questions

1. What do you understand the purpose or mission of your department to be?

2. Tell me how well you think your department is structured to accomplish its mission effectively.
3. Tell me how you allocate your time among the various tasks you do each day.
4. How well are you able to utilize your skills and abilities in your present job?
5. How would you characterize the contribution you're now making to your department?
6. Are there any functions you are now performing that could be reduced or eliminated?
7. What input do you have into the way decisions are made in your department?
8. How do you feel about your opportunities for growth and development on the job?
9. Do you know how well you are performing on your job? How do you know?
10. Do you know what is expected of you on the job? How do you know?
11. What kind of recognition do you get for the work you do? From whom?
12. What are your aspirations for the future?
13. Do you feel that work is allocated properly in your department?
14. Are there any circumstances that keep you from performing your job as you would like?
15. In the past year (six months, month) what accomplishment could you point to as an example of your skill and expertise?
16. Tell me about a project or task that didn't go entirely as you wished. What were the problems? How did you try to solve them?
17. Do you work best alone or as a member of a team? Tell me why?
18. If we added employees to your group, describe the kind of person we should hire.
19. How are you like or unlike that person?
20. What things seem to be changing about the way you do your job or about your work situation here? How do you feel about those changes?
21. How do you feel about the way you are managed?

22. How do you manage your subordinates?
23. How would you characterize your relations with fellow employees?
24. How do you know when you've done a good job?
25. What would you like to change most about your work situation?

FIGURE H–2
Performance Appraisal Record

Interviewee's Name: Date: Interviewer:

Objectives Met and Unmet
Attitudes Expressed
Use of Time
Relations with Others
Work Quality/Quantity
Employee Development
Agreed-upon Short- and Long-term Goals

THE EXIT INTERVIEW

Approximately 40 percent of American corporations, large and small, conduct exit interviews as a regular part of the personnel process. An exit interview is a nondefensive, nonjudgmental conversation with employees leaving the company. Ideally, the interview is conducted by someone other than the employee's direct supervisor or a superior who will later be used as a reference.

Goals

• To learn the exiting employee's perceptions of strengths and weaknesses within the company, including attitudes toward salary, benefits, supervision, work assignments, company leadership, and work conditions.
• To understand why the employee is attracted to other companies, perhaps competitors.
• To establish or maintain favorable relations between the company and exiting employees, many of whom will return to the company at a later date or who will make recommendations to friends about employment there.

Common Problems

• The exiting employee is interviewed by his or her immediate supervisor or a superior who will later be used as a job reference. In the first case, the employee may be unable to discuss the real problems on the job—especially when those problems directly involved the personality, management style, or intelligence of the supervisor. In the second case, the employee may hold back frank opinions for fear of alienating a superior who may later act as a recommender.
• Topics are phrased in a threatening, punitive, or judgmental way. It does little good to ask an employee, "What could you have done to make your stay here more successful?" The exiting employee, after all, has little motivation to answer such questions—he or she is

leaving. Questions must be phrased (as in the examples below) so that the employee is made to feel like a helpful consultant to the company, not a naughty child.

• Questions are not open enough to let the exiting employee have his or her say. Too often exit interviewers assume that they know why employees are leaving. Favorite reasons are salary, work load, or better opportunities. Interviewers have a tendency, in such cases, to limit discussion entirely to those topics. As a result, exiting employees may not get a chance to explain their real feelings with regard to their work experience.

• The interviewer fails to explain what use will be made of the opinions given by the employee. Ideally, all exit interview data should be treated anonymously. If an exiting employee gives supervisors or co-workers negative evaluations, he or she should not have to worry about being "blackballed" in the profession by those people. To create a climate in which the exiting employee will speak freely, the interview must make explicit assurances regarding the anonymity, confidentiality, and method of recording and using the opinions given. The following is a sample assurance statement.

> Bob, we appreciate this chance to get your thoughts and feelings about the company. Everything we discuss in the next half hour will be confidential and anonymous. You're not being recorded. The only notes I'm making are for our statistical use in determining where the company is doing well and where it needs to improve. Your name will not be attached to any of the opinions you give.

Sample Questions

1. Tell me about your salary history with the company.
2. How fairly were you treated with regard to salary by the company?
3. How often and on what basis was your performance evaluated?
4. How fair was the evaluation, in your opinion?
5. Share with me your attitudes about the benefits package at the company.
6. Which benefits mattered most to you? Which mattered least?
7. How did you feel about your physical working conditions at the company?

8. How did you feel about your social working conditions, including your co-workers and supervisors?
9. How appropriate was your workload, given your skills and level of experience? Did you have enough to do? Too much? Too little?
10. Within your work group, how fairly was work distributed, in your opinion?
11. What is your attitude toward your climb up the ladder during your time with the company? Did you make the progress you wished?
12. Tell me about any barriers that you felt were holding you back from achieving your goals with the company.
13. How would you describe you own feelings or morale toward your job? Toward the company?
14. What seemed to be the feelings or morale of others you worked with toward their jobs? Toward the company?
15. In your opinion, how could the company improve morale among the work force?
16. Tell me about your relations with co-workers.
17. Tell me about your relations with your supervisor.
18. Tell me about your relations with your subordinates.
19. What changes would you recommend to improve operations in your work unit? In the company?
20. In your opinion, what would make this company more competitive?
21. What company policies or procedures did you dislike? Why?
22. In looking for employment elsewhere, what were the primary factors that attracted you to another position?
23. What aspects of this job will you be glad to leave behind?
24. What advice would you have for senior management here?
25. What other topics do you feel we should discuss? (Or, what other topics would you ask an exiting employee to discuss?)

FIGURE H–3
Exit Interview Record

Employee's Name:

Employee's Number:

Date of Birth:

Title:

Type of employment: ( ) Full-time ( ) Part-time ( ) Salaried
( ) Hourly

Company unit, group, or division:

Department:

Physical location:

Last phone number:

Date hired:

Grade or level:

Ending base salary:

Date of termination:

Circumstances of termination: (layoff?   resigned?   release?
other?)

Total time in present job:

Primary duties:

Immediate manager/supervisor:

Name or type of company for new job:

New job title:

New base pay:

What are the exiting employee's attitudes about each of the
following?

• *salary in the job being left*
• *benefits*

- *distribution of work*
- *personal work load*
- *progress in the company*
- *morale among employees*
- *methods of management and supervision used by company*
- *relationship with immediate supervisor or manager*
- *relationship with upper management*
- *relationship with peers*
- *relationship with subordinates*
- *company policies, procedures, or practices (include any recommended changes)*

Comments:

Interviewer's Signature:

Date:

THE COUNSELING INTERVIEW

The purpose of this interview is two-fold: to uncover career-related personal or interpersonal problems and to guide the interviewee toward a resolution of those problems. While all counseling deals to some degree with psychological issues, the following discussion focusses on the counseling interview in a business environment, not in a medical or psychotherapeutic context.

Goals

• To create an atmosphere of trust in which deep-seated and potentially threatening topics or attitudes can be discussed.
• To understand topics and problems discussed from the interviewee's point of view.
• To lead the interviewee to courses of thought and action that will prove personally and professionally beneficial. (The interviewer achieves this goal primarily through active listening, empathy, and information sharing.)

Common Problems

• The interviewee feels that his or her opinions don't matter. The counseling interview cannot succeed if it is viewed (by interviewer or interviewee) as a lecture session. While the interviewer often has company-approved ends in mind for the interview, those goals should not be imposed in such a way as to squelch expression of feelings or exploration of alternatives.
• The interviewee doesn't trust the interviewer. Truly volatile personal or interpersonal issues are difficult to discuss with even close friends, much less a counselor in the workplace. Inevitably a certain degree of highly personal information—marriage, self-image, health fears, and so forth—come up during the counseling interview. The interviewer must therefore be explicit in assuring the interviewee

that the session is confidential. For this reason, companies have had little luck in asking supervisors and managers to double as counseling interviewers. They are usually too involved in the politics and power of the work environment to be "trustable" by those counseled. Instead, companies employ professionally trained counselors to handle these interviews.

• The interviewer is powerless within the organization to do anything about the dilemmas discussed by the interviewee. When an interviewee spills his or her deepest thoughts and feelings about a work situation, it's not enough for the interviewer to say, in effect, "Well, do the best you can"—thereby putting the burden for change entirely on the interviewee. Counseling interviewers should have direct communication, with necessary clout, to all levels of management within the company. The goal, after all, is to resolve problems, not merely share them.

Sample Assurance of Confidentiality

Linda, we're here to discuss the obvious problems that have been occurring between you and Ms. Johnson, your supervisor. Before we begin, I want you to know that anything you tell me will be handled confidentially. I won't report anything you say to Ms. Johnson or anyone else without your permission.

Sample Statement of Purpose

Mike, we're meeting to see if we can get to the root of the morale problem among your employees. I'm not interested in placing blame— I just want to understand how you view the situation and to see if together we can find a solution.

Sample Questions (If a particular situation is at issue, substitute it wherever "the problem" is mentioned below.)

1. Tell me what you think we should talk about.
2. How do you feel about this discussion? Do you think it can help?
3. What could we do in the next half hour (hour, etc.) to get to the heart of the matter?

4. Tell me about some of the personalities involved in the problem.
5. Tell me specifically what others do that upsets you. Describe your feelings as completely as you can.
6. I can understand your feelings of anger. Tell me how you express those feelings.
7. Things obviously aren't the way you would like them to be. Describe for me how things should be.
8. Start from the beginning and tell me how the problem developed.
9. What do you think your supervisor (co-worker, etc.) expects of you?
10. How do you feel about those expectations?
11. In what ways should you have been treated differently by others?
12. If you had complete control over this situation, what would you do?
13. This may be difficult, but I'd like you to try to describe the problem from the other person's point of view.
14. In most problems, there are spectators and participants. In this problem, who are the spectators—people on the sidelines watching the struggle? Who are the participants battling it out on the field?
15. Do you leave these feelings at work each day or take them home with you?
16. Give me a "worst case scenario" for this problem. How bad can it get? What will you do then?
17. What do you think caused the problem?
18. With whom do you share your feelings about this problem? What do they say?
19. You said there were good days and bad days with regard to this problem. Tell me what makes for a good day? What makes a bad day?
20. Once I completely understand your point of view, what do you think I should do?
21. I'm going to say back to you a few of the key words you've used to describe the problem. For each word, tell me what thoughts or feelings you have. (Proceed to say back key words—for example, "hostility," "insubordination," "attitude problem," "smart aleck.")

22. This problem has kept you from doing some of the things you want to do. What are some of those things?
23. If (name a party to the problem) were sitting here with us, what would you say to him or her?
24. Let's reverse roles. Ask me the question that matters most in this problem.
25. As you look at the problem, what aspects are within your own power to solve? What aspects are out of your power?

FIGURE H–4
Counseling Interview Record

Interviewee's Name: Date: Interviewer:

Initial Impressions of Interviewee

Interviewee's Attitudes

Interviewee's Emotions

Interviewee's Perception of Problem(s)

Interviewee's Suggested Solution(s)

Notes and Comments

THE INFORMATION INTERVIEW

An information interview seeks to gather facts and sources for facts. It is typically used by a new manager getting "up to speed" on projects within the work unit; by media specialists within the company, gathering information for press releases, advertising, and training materials; and by financial personnel seeking data for budgeting and decision making.

Goals

• To collect facts in an organized way for later use in plannng, publications, training, or decision making.
• To determine sources for facts, including the relative authority and trustworthiness of those sources.

Common Problems

• Interviewees hold back information. Interviewers must explain their "need to know" with care and patience to encourage a free flow of information from interviewees. Knowledge in organizations, after all, is a form of power: what the boss knows can hurt you.
• Interviewers ask for facts in a disorganized manner. The "shotgun" approach to information seeking discourages full disclosure on the part of interviewees. Like a vein of ore, one line of questioning should be thoroughly explored before turning to another line. A technical question about wing stability, for example, should not be followed immediately by a question on overall funding for research and development. Interviewees will conclude that the interviewer doesn't know what he or she is asking or that the interviewer doesn't understand the significance of the answers received.
• Interviewers fail to record facts in a visible way. Especially where technical explanations and complicated descriptions are concerned, interviewees need to know that their words are being recorded

accurately. Too often interviewers simply nod "uh-huh" after an exhaustive rehearsal of facts by the interviewee. If no recording method (tape, notes, etc.) is present, the interviewee will tend to give more and more brief, simplistic answers.

Sample Statement of Purpose

In the next hour I'm going to ask you for information regarding the B-17 project. What you tell me is being recorded so that we can make a printed transcript. You'll have a chance to review the transcript and to make any changes before we use your information to plan training manuals.

Sample Questions (Substitute "this situation," "this proposal," "this product," or other phrase as appropriate in place of "this project.")

1. Tell me about the development of this project.
2. Tell me about the people involved in this project.
3. If the development of this project could be divided into stages, what would they be?
4. Tell me about the most difficult aspects of this project.
5. Tell me about how the client has responded to this project.
6. How would you describe this project to a 10-year-old child?
7. How does this project differ from _____
(fill in another project).
8. What financial information is available on this project?
9. What risks does the company run in backing this project?
10. What risks do employees run in working on the project?
11. How will the project look to us in two (three, five) years?
12. How is the project like other projects completed by the company?
13. What basic facts should I know about the materials used in the project?
14. What are the costs, including projected future costs, of those materials?
15. How is the project managed? By whom?
16. What are the milestones for project completion and implementation? How were those milestones determined?
17. How will we measure the relative success of the project?

18. What is the essential value of the project? (to the company, to society, etc.)
19. What is the reputation of the project? (in the profession, in the company, among the public, etc.)
20. Who are the most knowledgeable about the project?
21. How is the development of the project being recorded or tracked?
22. On what technologies does the success of the project depend?
23. On what social attitudes does the success of the project depend?
24. What will motivate end-users to buy (participate in, sponsor, fund) the project?
25. What aspects of the project must be considered proprietary?

FIGURE H–5
Information Interview Record

Interviewee's Name:	Date:	Interviewer:

History

Divisions

Problem Areas

Marketing

Technical Information

Present Status

Financial Information

Milestones

Administration/Management

Key Personnel and Contacts

Notes and Comments

THE NEGOTIATION INTERVIEW

In the negotiation interview, parties with opposed interests and points of view join in an effort to reach a mutually agreeable compromise. Negotiation interviews are common in labor/management situations, vendor/purchaser price conferences, and contract discussions.

Goals

• To maximize what is in the interest of both parties while minimizing what is in the interest of neither party or only one party.
• To build understanding and relations conducive to working among parties.

Common Problems

• Negotiators can be blinded by ego. Particularly in heated negotiation interviews, participants can be heard to grumble "You can't do that to me." They have so deeply internalized their mission that an objection to an idea or proposal becomes an objection to their person. Negotiators must learn, through training and experience, not to take heated objections personally.
• Negotiators quit talking. The game of negotiation involves "tough stands," "final offers," and "absolute courses of action" that really are far from tough, final, or absolute. Both sides to the negotiation bluster and bluff as a way of determining just how much the opponent is willing to give. Negotiations fail, therefore, when negotiators end discussion as soon as such bluffs occur. A continuing dialogue can often reach compromises that seemed impossible at earlier stages in negotiation.
• Negotiators go back on their word. Progress in negotiations usually happens verbally—one side is willing to go on to certain compromises based on verbal concessions made by the other side. Trust and the possibility for compromise break down, however, when one side

"forgets" or goes back on its verbal assurances. To prevent such backtracking, all major points in the negotiation process should be set down in writing, then signed off by participants. While such a signoff procedure usually does not have true contractual status, it does help to avoid the "but-you-said, no-we-didn't" problem in verbal negotiation.

Sample Statement of Purpose

We're all here because there are substantial profits to be made on all sides by a mutually agreeable contract. We have different attitudes toward what that contract should contain. But in the coming hours and days, we should not lose track of our goal: finding terms to give us all a strong incentive to sign the final contract.

Sample Questions

1. What portion of our proposal can you agree with?
2. With what specific aspects of our proposal do you disagree? Why?
3. What counterproposal can you offer?
4. What do our proposals have in common? How do they differ?
5. Of the items with which you disagree, which matter to you most? Which least?
6. In what areas do you think compromise is most easily reached?
7. In difficult areas of compromise, what trade-offs are possible?
8. What historical (social, political, etc.) reasons help to explain your strong stand on _____ (some aspect of their proposal).
9. What do you want to understand more about in our proposal?
10. How would our proposal, if agreed upon, affect your people?
11. What do we have to lose if we fail to reach an agreement?
12. How much time can pass before any agreement becomes impossible or irrelevant?
13. Tell us what you think should be included in an ideal compromise.

14. What are your primary goals in this agreement? What goals are secondary?
15. What are your greatest concerns with this agreement as it now stands?
16. What do your people expect from you when you come out of this negotiation?
17. What do your superiors expect from you when you come out of this negotiation?
18. What kind of time frame should we be working within to reach an agreement?
19. What issues can we discuss on an individual basis? Can we separate them out for agreement prior to reaching an agreement on the overall proposal?
20. Of the points we've agreed to discuss, what priority should we follow?
21. What incentive would you require to agree with certain aspects of our proposal?
22. How much consultation with your people will be required for you to go forward with points of agreement?
23. Can we reach a final agreement by setting aside issues on which we disagree for later discussion?
24. Would a break be helpful as a period during which to consider certain points?
25. Now that we've reached a compromise, what is the best way to announce and implement our agreement?

FIGURE H–6
Negotiation Interview Record

Interviewee's Name:	Date:	Interviewer:

Brief Description of Negotiation Goals

Areas of Agreement

Areas of Disagreement

Possible Trade-offs

Strategies

Progress

Time Frame for Decisions/Agreement

Notes and Comments

THE PERSUASION/
SALES INTERVIEW

This common interview occurs whenever one party tries to guide another toward a desired course of thinking or action through questions and discusion. Among the many types of persuasion/sales interviews are the transfer/new responsibilities interview, in which a manager tries to persuade a subordinate to willingly take another position or new responsibilites in the company; the resources interview, in which a manager apportions or seeks funding; and the client interview, in which the salesperson determines the client's needs and how they can be met.

Goals

• To convince the interviewee of the desirability of a course of action or thinking.
• To overcome objections to that course of action or thinking.
• To build ongoing interpersonal relationships conducive to problem solving.

Common Problems

• The interviewer knows the answer but the interviewee doesn't know the question. Some persuaders, caught up in the enthusiasm of their product and "pitch," forget to solicit the interviewee's needs and attitudes. Even the most polished persuasional or sales approach will fall on deaf ears under these circumstances.
• The inteviewee is asked too soon for a decision. Particularly in complex matters such as new job responsibilities or financial decisions, interviewees need time to come to terms with new ideas.
• The interviewee doesn't have a chance to ask questions. Many people in sales are by nature, both assertive and controlling. They like to take a stand, overcome objections, and come out the winner. As positive as these qualities are for success in sales, they must

not smother the interviewee's chance to ask questions. "I know what you're thinking" goes the typical sales pitch. But interviewees appreciate a less presumptuous approach—one that sincerely asks what they're thinking.

Sample Questions (Substitute "process,"
"person," "promotion," or "policy"
in place of "product" as appropriate.)

1. In trying to achieve your goals, what product have you tried?
2. How did that product work out?
3. What would you have changed in that product?
4. What did your people have to say about the product?
5. If you had continued to use the product, what would have been the result?
6. What contact did you have with those who made the product? What was your feeling about that contact?
7. What kind of product do you need?
8. What other needs may develop for you in the future?
9. How would you like to interface with the supplier of the product?
10. What should the product do for you?
11. What should the product be careful not to do?
12. How much do you want to pay for the product?
13. How much would you be willing to pay for a product that met your needs entirely?
14. How much product will you require?
15. By what process will you determine which product to buy?
16. How will you decide how well you like the product?
17. Who in your company will be in charge of using the product?
18. What experience or background do you require in those using the product?
19. Where will the product be used?
20. What are your short-term (long-term) business goals?
21. How can we assist you in reaching those goals?
22. When will you decide which product to buy?
23. What interests you about our product?
24. What concerns you most about the purchase or use of our product?
25. What questions do you have about our product or service?

FIGURE H–7
Persuasion/Sales Interview Record

Interviewee's Name: Date: Interviewer:

Interviewee's Needs and Goals
Products Tried, with Reaction
Interviewee's Description of Ideal Product
Areas of Resistance to Our Product
Key Points in Overcoming Resistance
Benefits to Interviewee (include Supplier services)
Specific Product Requirements (volume, date, type)
Future Needs
Notes and Comments

THE DISCIPLINARY INTERVIEW

This interview, in many ways the most difficult of all, takes place both formally and informally in business. It ranges from the staged dressing-down of a senior manager before the CEO or board of directors to the quick, in-the-hall reprimand for a long-lunching employee.

Goals

• To change undesirable behavior through constructive questions and discussion.
• To maintain and even increase good working relations between superior and subordinates.

Common Problems

• Those disciplined misunderstand criticism as a personal attack. "Hate the sin, not the sinner," goes the old Methodist saying. Questions and assertions in a disciplinary interview must be phrased carefully so that the individual does not feel demeaned or disliked. The reason for such care is obvious: an individual can hope to change aspects of behavior but wilts at the thought of having to become an entirely different person to please the boss.
• The interviewer fails to hear the other side of the story. Even in open/shut cases of policy or procedure violation, a manager should take time to ask for and listen to the disciplined person's side of the story. Often that version will contribute valuable information on how the problem can be avoided in the future.
• The interview concludes on a negative note. If, in fact, the goal of the disciplinary interview is to change behavior, then the end of that interview should emphasize benefits of "doing it right" next time. The disciplined person, understanding his or her mistakes, should then be motivated to work toward positive goals. The agony of defeat, in other words, has to accompanied by the thrill of victory.

Sample Introduction to the Disciplinary Interview

Herb, I want to talk to you about your behavior in the office toward female employees. What we'll discuss won't go into your file at this point and won't leave this office. But I'm deeply concerned about the situation I've observed and heard about. I want to hear your perspective and come up with solutions.

Sample Questions

1. Why do you think you're here for this discussion?
2. What is your side of the story?
3. Have you experienced problems such as this before? When? What were the circumstances?
4. Why do you think the problem occurred?
5. What, in your view, would have prevented the problem?
6. Why don't others you work with have this problem?
7. Are others to blame that I should know about? What did they do?
8. If you were in my position, how would you handle this situation?
9. What were the specific details of the situation as you remember them?
10. Why did the problem occur when it did and not before?
11. Are there similar problems that I should know about?
12. Who knows about this problem? How did they respond?
13. Will the problem occur again in the future? If not, what will prevent it?
14. Are you aware of the company's usual procedures for dealing with this problem? If so, what are they?
15. Are there reasons why these procedures should not be applied to you? If so, what are those reasons?
16. What could the company do to prevent this problem from occurring again?
17. Do you think others are likely to have this problem? Why? What can the company do to help?
18. What are you willing to do to make up for this problem?
19. How do you feel about your future in this company?
20. What will you do to keep this problem from recurring?

21. In your opinion, what has been the impact of this problem on the company? On your co-workers? On your career?
22. What special circumstances should I know about before deciding what to do about this problem?
23. When did you first discover that the problem had come to light? How did you respond?
24. Were the policies and procedures of the company clearly communicated to you during your employment? If not, what did you misunderstand?
25. Are there questions about this discussion or about the problem that you would like to ask me?

FIGURE H–8
Disciplinary Interview Record

Interviewee's Name: Date: Interviewer:

Problem Description and History

Interviewee's Initial Attitudes

Information/Explanation Volunteered Regarding Problem

Interviewee's Suggested Solution

Others Allegedly Involved

Impact of Problem on Work Unit, Company, Clients

Interviewee's Exiting Attitudes

Notes and Comments

THE CAREER-PLANNING
INTERVIEW

This interview is carried on extensively both on high school and college campuses as well as in business. Some interviews involve a battery of written tests designed to measure, with validated accuracy, areas of special talent and skill.

Goals

- To match a person's preferences, experience, and abilities with job tasks.
- To assist the person in making personal decisions with regard to career choices.
- To make the best possible use of company personnel through effective career guidance.

Common Problems

- The interviewee feels pigeonholed. There is a natural tendency to label and categorize people: Joe is a computer type, Mary is a natural trainer, Frank is a born manager, and so forth. These stereotypes must be left at the door in a successful career-planning interview. Proper career choices emerge only when the spectrum of choices is as unrestricted as possible.
- The interviewer plays God. On the slimmest of verbal and even nonverbal evidence, the interviewer may pronounce, "No, I don't think you're the type to pursue a career in finance." How does the interviewer know? By an untied shoelace, supposedly indicating inattention to detail? These "seat-of-the-pants" judgments must be suppressed, especially when dealing with relatively impressionable young adults.
- The interviewee is given a plethora of choices but no basis on which to make a final choice. Variety of choices is not necessarily freedom of choice; at times variety alone can produce paralysis of decision

making. The career interviewer should show the interviewee not only what's available but also what factors he or she should consider in making a choice. Some of these factors are work conditions, the degree to which tasks are structured, the amount and type of supervision, the nature of and need for feedback, and so forth. These form the criteria by which the interviewee can eventually come to firm personal decisions.

Sample Questions

1. What do you do well?
2. What do others say about your work?
3. What is your idea of an ideal job?
4. What do you like most about your present job? What do you like least?
5. How do you feel about the tasks you're now asked to do?
6. Describe your supervisor's management style. How does he or she direct your work? How do you feel about that form of supervision?
7. How are you most like your co-workers? How are you most unlike them?
8. What tasks are you most prepared to do by your education?
9. What tasks are you most prepared to do by your experience?
10. If your friends had to pick a proper job for you, what would it be?
11. Tell me about a recent task you worked on. How did you feel about it?
12. Describe to me where you see yourself professionally in three (five, ten) years. Give me a good idea of what you're thinking and feeling about yourself at that time.
13. Name someone you admire in the company. Why do you admire them? In what ways would you like to be like them?
14. Name two or three jobs you would hate to do. What do they all have in common that you dislike?
15. Tell me about your interpersonal abilities. How do you get along with people? How do people feel about you?
16. Imagine that you supervise the work of ten other people. What problems do you think would come your way in the first year?

17. How do you think a manager should motivate people who work for him or her?
18. Name two or three jobs you might like to have. What do they all have in common?
19. What barriers get in your way as you try to accomplish your own goals in your present job? How do you deal with those barriers?
20. Do you feel appreciated for what you do now? How is that appreciation expressed. If no appreciation is expressed, how do you think it should be expressed?
21. How valuable do you think you are to the company? What would make you even more valuable?
22. What are your financial goals? Are you meeting your financial objectives for this period in your life?
23. What balance do you try to keep between work and play in your life? How well are you keeping that balance in your present job?
24. What would you like to accomplish most in your lifetime?
25. What puzzles you most about yourself?

FIGURE H–9
Career Planning Interview Record

Interviewee's Name: Date: Interviewer:

Job History

Interviewee's Assessment of Abilities

Interviewee's Description of Ideal Job

Areas of Possible Misassessment/Self-delusion

Future Goals, including Financial

Social Skills, Attitudes

Notes and Comments

THE FOCUS GROUP
INTERVIEW

In development, survey, and marketing situations, focus groups are used more and more as an efficient way to pretest ideas and products. In effect, a cross section of likely users (or experts in user needs) are assembled for an in-depth review of a new concept, product, or service. The feedback accumulated through this interview determines revision and development plans.

Goals

• To expose a new idea, service, or product in a relatively unstructured way to a selected audience.
• To gather responses, attitudes, and insights from a target audience through questions and discussion.

Common Problems

• The focus group feels constrained to be extreme in judgments. Particularly when group members are paid for their participation (as is usually the case), they feel pressure to "do a really good job." For some, this means adopting a hypercritical attitude; they have dozens of suggestions for improving the item at hand. For others, payment brings on an attack of niceness: the product or idea is praised to the skies. Both responses are less than useful. The sponsor of the focus group wants to know how people think and feel, not how they think they should think and feel.
• The focus group leader is dictatorial. Some leaders develop an extensive agenda of questions, then march through them—in checklist fashion—with the group barely keeping up. Group members find themselves nodding yes or no to the leader's assertions rather than giving opinions.

• The focus is out-of-focus. By contrast with the problem of dictatorship, some focus groups are left to wander through impressions without any guidance. Conversation strays to other products, industry issues, personal experiences, and everything except what the sponsor of the focus group wants: attitudes and responses that can be used for revision and final development.

Sample Introduction to a Focus Group

Thank you for giving us this hour to review our proposed table of contents for Dr. Smith's accounting textbook. I'll guide your attention to four main areas of interest, but along the way please feel free to add anything you wish or bring up new concerns.

Sample Questions

1. What do you see in this item that you like? Why?
2. What do you see here that you dislike? Why?
3. What aspects of this item seem especially useful?
4. To whom will this item appeal most? Least?
5. How large do you think the likely audience for this item will be?
6. What are the major competitors to this item?
7. In what ways is it better than the competition? Worse? About the same?
8. How much would you charge for this item?
9. What would be the best ways to advertise this product?
10. What should still be added to (or taken away from) this item?
11. What do you associate this item with? Why?
12. How well do you like the way this item is organized?
13. What do you see as disadvantages of using this item?
14. How would you improve this item?
15. Identify the possible uses you see for this item?
16. What do you like about competing products?
17. What do you dislike about competing products?
18. How easy would this product be to use?
19. What difficulties would you face in using this product?
20. What should accompany this item to make a complete package?

21. How do you feel about the design of this item?
22. Would you recommend this item to a friend? What would you tell him or her about it?
23. How long would you estimate the life expectancy of this item to be?
24. How would you introduce this item to the market?
25. What questions would you like to ask me about this item?

FIGURE H–10
Focus Group Interview Record

Group Names:	Date:	Interviewer:

Initial Impressions of Product

Suggested Market

Comparison to Competition

Revision Suggestions

Attitudes toward Use of Product

Estimates of Life Expectancy for Product

Suggestions for Introduction of Product

Notes and Comments

THE NEWS/PRESS
CONFERENCE INTERVIEW

This interview is usually conducted under the pressure of time. The interviewer may have to meet a deadline; the interviewee may have limited time at a press conference. As a result, questions must be direct and clear. The suggested questions in this section can be used at all levels of news interviewing, from politics to in-house newsletter reporting.

Goals

• To state questions of general interest in such a way that the interviewer must respond succinctly and candidly.
• To follow up on the implications or ambiguities of the interviewee's responses in order to draw out as definitive an answer as time will allow.

Common Problems

• The interviewee often controls the interviewer. In large press conferences, such as those conducted (occasionally) by the President, the point of a finger from the interviewee determines who will ask questions. Often favored reporters (and bland questioners) get called on again and again. Interviewers fight this tendency by behavior just at the edge of impertinence: they call out questions, poke arms in the air, and generally make themselves hard to ignore.
• Unfocussed questions allow the interviewee to escape difficult or uncomfortable answers. Questions beginning with "What do you have to say about" and "Can you comment on" are notoriously vague. The interviewee is usually free to respond by mentioning only the most favorable aspects of the topic. By contrast, questions beginning with "Did you" or "Is it true that" tend to pin the interviewee down to specific answers.

• Poor follow-up questions let the interviewee off the hook. When an interviewee hasn't answered the question or has tried to snow the audience with a blizzard of bureaucratic clichés, the interviewer must be ready with a brief, sharp follow-up question that points up the inadequacy of the first response and forces the interviewee to face the issue directly. Good follow-up questions often begin with "Please answer the question: Did you" or "Let me bring you back to the question: Is it true that."

Sample Questions (The questions below can be completed to fit varying topics and circumstances.)

1. Is it true that. . . ?
2. Did you. . . ?
3. How do you explain the fact that. . . ?
4. How do you respond to allegations that. . . ?
5. Why did you refuse to. . . ?
6. How do you justify your decision to. . . ?
7. Who is responsible for. . . ?
8. Who should take credit for. . . ?
9. What information can you give us about. . . ?
10. Are rumors true that the company. . . ?
11. Your critics claim that. . . How do you answer them?
12. Your supporters defend you by saying. . . . Is that your defense as well?
13. What will be the impact of your decision on. . . ?
14. How will this course of action affect. . . ?
15. How will you restructure the company in order to. . . ?
16. Who will be appointed to. . . ?
17. What do you plan to do about. . . ?
18. What were you trying to accomplish when you. . . ?
19. How do you answer charges that you. . . ?
20. From whom will you pick in choosing. . . ?
21. Whom will you consult in making your decision to. . . ?
22. When can we expect a decision on. . . ?
23. What do you say to people who complain that. . . ?
24. How much will it cost the company to. . . ?
25. How many workers will be affected by. . . ?

FIGURE H–11
News/Press Conference Interview Record

Interviewee's Name: Date: Interviewer:

Situation

Key Topics

Denials

Confirmations

Explanations

Accusations

Notes and Comments

THE BROADCAST INTERVIEW

Like the news/press conference interview, this form of question-and-answer emphasizes direct, germane questions. It differs from ordinary news reporting, however, in that the interviewer has more of a chance to establish a presence—a personality—along with the questions he or she asks. That presence can be confrontational, as in a Mike Wallace interview, or friendly and persuasive, after the fashion of Barbara Walters.

Goals

• To pose direct, relevant questions in an ordered way, linked by similarities in content or by conversational transitions.
• To use the relationship between interviewer and interviewee as a means to elicit candid answers, often in spite of the interviewee's conscious resistance.

Common Problems

• Interviewers fail to link their questions. When a broadcast interview devolves into a catechism session, with question after question fired in test fashion at the interviewee, the session loses its interpersonal and dramatic appeal. Shrewd interviewers do get to the questions they want to ask, but by building questions upon the responses given by the interviewee.
• Interviewers fail to show feeling. If an interviewee's response is vague and confusing, the questioner should express his or her confusion and rephrase the question. If the stonewalling of the interviewee proves frustrating, the interviewer should show those emotions, even if only by humorous reference ("I must admit, Senator, that I'm struggling to understand what you mean").
• Interviewees protect themselves by taking up large amounts of time on easy, safe questions. Interviewers must be ready to cut in when

an interviewee has passed the "meat" of the answer and has moved on to the fat. Often a quick, curt compliment can stop a flood of superfluous words: "Thank you for explaining that. Now let me ask you—".

Sample Questions

The heart of good broadcast interview questions are to be found in the news/press conference questions above. But notice in this treatment of the first five of those questions how the interviewer's personality and feelings play a powerful role in eliciting candid answers.

1. You were a sponsor, Senator, of a highly praised bill last year—the Truth in Government Act. In the spirit of that bill, let me ask you: Is it true that. . . ?

2. Maybe I'm not hearing what you're saying. Did you. . . ?

3. The examples you've given were carried in most papers, including mine. But how do you explain the fact that. . . ?

4. It's no secret that you have strong opinions when it comes to your political enemies. But, aside from blaming partisanship, how do you respond to allegations that. . . ?

5. One thing that has confused many of us in the press corps is your stand on abortion. Why did you refuse to. . . ?

THE TELEPHONE AND TELECONFERENCE INTERVIEW

All of the interviews above can be handled, with varying effectiveness, on the telephone. When conducting telephone interviews, however, certain guidelines must be kept in mind:

• Your voice must carry signals of friendliness, interest, and involvement that your nonverbal signals—expression, eyes, hands, posture and so forth—express when you interview in person. So that long periods of listening aren't interpreted by your interviewee as cold, judgmental silence, insert nonobtrusive expressions of interest: "Uh-hum," "I see," "Yes," and so forth. These are not necessarily expressions of agreement. You're simply indicating that you're listening intently.

• Speak even more distinctly than usual. Even with ideal telephone transmission, the interviewee can't get additional help in understanding your words from seeing your lips, gestures, or expressions.

• Ask questions that can be answered briefly. By convention, we're not used to lecturing one another on the telephone. Your interviewee will feel uncomfortable giving sustained answers that last more than 30 to 45 seconds. In the case of complex questions, therefore, break them up into separate parts. Let your interviewee know you wish to take one part at a time.

• Don't prolong the phone interview for more than 10 to 15 minutes. This figure, of course, is a general approximation of the "lasting power" of interviewees on the telephone. The same person who shows pleasure talking to you in person for an hour will probably begin to wilt after 15 minutes on the phone. We are generally unaccustomed, after all, to speaking for long periods by telephone. We have to hold a relatively rigid physical posture, with receiver clamped to the ear. Plan interview questions, therefore, so that the most crucial issues are treated in the first 10 minutes.

Questions for Self-Assessment of In-Depth Interviewing

The following questions provide useful windows for assessing your own habits and attitudes. Many of the questions can also be used for in-depth business interviews, including selection interviews for managerial and other "high-touch" positions.

The questions are best answered on a 5-point scale, ranging from "Definitely Yes" to "Definitely No."

Definitely Yes   Definitely No

5	4	3	2	1

1. Are most of your friends warm?
2. Do you make excuses for or allowances for friends more than for others?
3. Are you depressed for at least a few days each month?
4. Do you spend more freely than you should, based on your income?
5. Do you tell the truth to your friends?
6. Do you tell the truth to mere acquaintances?
7. When you disagree with someone, do you find it hard to believe he or she can't see the wisdom of your position?
8. Do you usually take action rather than waiting for events to occur?
9. Do you spend much time playing worries over and over in your head?
10. Do you stand up well under pressure?
11. Is your judgment influenced often by your emotions?
12. Do you usually find yourself busy with too many interests at once?
13. Do you put off bothersome but necessary tasks?
14. Do you take a strong, single stand on most issues?
15. Do you often touch friends in the course of greeting them or saying goodbye?
16. Do you find it easy to relax?
17. Do you think people talk behind your back frequently?
18. Do you laugh out loud very often?
19. Are you easily irritated by children?
20. Can you work efficiently in the presence of noise?

21. Do you talk less than most of your friends?
22. Do you believe that you have one or two major problems that keep holding you back?
23. When you have a complaint, do you always express it in a strong, direct way?
24. Do you find yourself following the crowd in spite of your own values or desires?
25. Does stress seem to bring on physical illness for you?
26. Do you have nervous physical habits, such as nail chewing?
27. Do you misplace or lose things often?
28. Do you "borrow" small items from your work, not planning to return them?
29. Do you plan carefully for events well before they occur?
30. Do you find yourself thinking often of death?
31. Are you a spectator more often than a participant in sports?
32. Do you consider yourself to be in good physical shape?
33. Do you have a few things you hate or fear?
34. Do people consider you easy-going?
35. Do you spend a great deal of time in conversation analyzing and criticizing others?
36. Do you spend time thinking about past mistakes?
37. Has your life gone pretty much the way you would have wished?
38. Do you often keep your opinions to yourself?
39. Does your mood change dramatically when you're tired?
40. Do you act on impulse more often than by plan?
41. Do you have occasional days that seem absolutely perfect?
42. Do you "shoot off your mouth" at times, later to regret it?
43. Do you handle failure well?
44. Do you keep peace at times by taking blame that isn't really yours?
45. Are you happy more than three-fourths of your waking hours?
46. Do you think about the pain experienced by animals prepared as food?
47. Do you tend to "work the room" at social gatherings?
48. Do you reach firm opinions only after considering the pros and cons of an issue?
49. Do you find it easy to communicate with people?
50. Do you "stick your foot in your mouth" often?

REFERENCES

Ahearn, Michael. Quoted in "Peopling a Business." *Fortune*, December 8, 1986, p. 203.

Baldridge, Letitia. Quoted in "The Right Way to Interview." *Savvy*, December 1985, p. 18.

Berger, Raymond M. Quoted in "Recruitment." *Personnel Journal*, February 1987, p. 91.

Bradley, Bob. Personal interview, June 1988.

Brennan, Vincent F. Quoted in "Don't Be Age Biased Against the Young or Old." *Working Woman*, October 1987, p. 28

Cabot, Stephen. Quoted in "Loaded Questions. . . Help to Hire the Best." *Industry Week*, January 21, 1985, p. 44, and in "The Educated Hunch." *INC.*, January, 1985 p. 94.

DiGeso, Amy. Quoted in "Career Workshop." *Working Woman*, June 1987, p. 87.

Einstein, Kurt. *Drake Performance Seminar*. 1987, p. 19.

Friedman, Robert B. Quoted in "Hiring the Best." *Nation's Business*, October 1987, p. 71.

Gilbert, Lynn. Quoted in "Surviving the Group Interview." *Forbes*, March 24, 1986, p. 190.

Gleeson, Marji. Quoted in "The Right Way to Interview." *Savvy*, December 1985, p. 18.

Half, Robert. Quoted in "How to Pick Talent." *Fortune*, December 8, 1986, p. 203, and in "Revealing Questions: A Guide for Job Interviewers." *Working Woman*, November 1985, p. 60.

Hopkins, John T. Quoted in "The Top Twelve Questions for Employment Agency Interviews." *Personnel Journal*, May 1980, p. 380.

Kiechell, Walter III. "How to Pick Talent." *Fortune*, December 8, 1986, p. 201.

Latterell, Jeffrey D. "Planning for the Selection Interview." *Personnel Journal*, July 1979, p. 466.

Loretto, Vincent. "Effective Interviewing Is Based on More Than Intuition." *Personnel Journal*, December 1986, p. 101.

Lynch, Dale. Personal interview, February 1988.

Melohn, Thomas. "Screening for the Best Employees." *INC.*, January 1987, p. 104.

Meyer, Sandra. Quoted in "Selling the Job." *Working Woman*, June 1987, p. 111.

McCoy, Millie. Quoted in "When You Are Doing the Hiring." *Working Woman*, February 1985, p. 48.

Nagel, Bob. Quoted in "Recruiting's Finest Hour: the Interview." *Supervisory and Management Monthly*, August 17, 1981, p. 59.

Oliver, Adela. Quoted in "Surviving the Group Interview." *Forbes*, March 24, 1986, p. 191.

Pedersen, Alan. Quoted in "The Educated Hunch." *INC.*, January 1985, p. 93.

Reynolds, Russell S., Jr. "How to Pick a New Executive. " September 1, 1986, *Fortune*, p. 113.

Richardson, Linda. Quoted in "Selling the Job." *Working Woman*, June 1987, p. 111.

Sargent, Jon. Quoted in "Money Management Financial Planners: How to Pick the Best for You." *Changing Times*, June 1986, p. 32.

Sherwood, Andrew. "Exit Interviews: Don't Just Say Goodbye." *Personnel Journal*, September 1983, p. 744-750.

Simpson, Larry. Quoted in "Adventures in the Retail Trade." *Forbes*, February 24, 1986, p. 122.

Slowik, Stanley. "Ask the Right Questions, Get the Right Answers." *Security Management*, March 1987, p. 75.

Smith, Fred. "Hiring: What Will It Cost You?" *Business-to-Business*, August 1987, p. 28.

Tucker, Donna H. "Recruitment." *Personnel Journal*, February 1987, p. 91.

Westerfield, Putney. Quoted in "Surviving the Group Interview." *Forbes*, March 24, 1986, p. 191.

Williams, McDonald. Quoted in "The New Art of Hiring Smart." *Fortune*, August 17, 1987, p. 79.

Winthrop, Laurie. Quoted in "The Right Way to Interview." *Savvy*, December 1985, p. 18.

Witkin, Arthur A. "Commonly Overlooked Dimensions of Employee Selection." *Personnel Journal*, July 1980, p. 573.

Young, William J. Quoted in "Finding the Right Job." *Glamour*, August 1984, p. 158.

INDEX